I Am
Annie
Mae

I am

UNIVERSITY OF TEXAS PRESS

AUSTIN

Annie Mae

AN EXTRAORDINARY
BLACK TEXAS WOMAN
IN HER OWN WORDS

BY ANNIE MAE HUNT
AND RUTHE WINEGARTEN
ASSISTANT EDITOR FRIEDA WERDEN

Book design: Eje W. Wray

Cover photograph of Annie Mae Hunt during the Depression,
from Hunt scrapbook

First University of Texas Press edition, 1996
Published by agreement with Ruthe Winegarten

♾ The paper used in this publication meets the minimum
requirements of American National Standard for Information
Sciences—Permanence of Paper for Printed Library Materials,
ANSI Z39.48-1984.

Library of Congress Cataloging-in-Publication Data

Hunt, Annie Mae, 1909–
    I am Annie Mae : an extraordinary Black Texas woman in her own
words / by Annie Mae Hunt and Ruthe Winegarten ; assistant editor, Frieda
Werden. — 1st University of Texas Press ed.
        p.   cm.
Originally published: Austin : Rosegarden Press, 1983.
Includes bibliographical references.
ISBN 0-292-79099-6 (pbk. : alk. paper)
1. Hunt, Annie Mae, 1909–   . 2. Afro-American women—Texas.
3. Texas—Biography.   I. Winegarten, Ruthe.   II. Werden, Frieda.
III. Title.
E185.93.T4H864   1996
976.4'00496073'0092—dc20
[B]   95-52883

I want to dedicate this book to my grandmother,
Matilda Boozie Randon, and my mother,
Callie Randon McDade.

> —Annie Mae Hunt

CONTENTS

Autograph party hosted by
former State Rep. Eddie
Bernice Johnson, right

Dallas

TV interview

Dallas Morning News

PREFACE

An "impertinent" remark made by young Annie Mae Hunt's stepdaddy to a white East Texas plantation owner in 1922 provoked a brutal attack on her mother, sister, and herself. Annie Mae Hunt's handwritten, partly finished manuscript of that account, begun when she was only 14, lay untouched in a cardboard box for over 50 years. During numerous moves, she carried that story with her, determined to bear witness some day. In 1977, introduced by a mutual friend, Mrs. Hunt and I signed a partnership contract to complete her work. I taped interviews with her over a five-year period, and together we published *I Am Annie Mae.*

The book was launched on June 3, 1983, at the American Booksellers Convention in Dallas. The response, both to the book and to Mrs. Hunt, has been overwhelming. The first printing of 1000 copies was sold out in three months, following dozens of newspaper and magazine articles, TV and radio appearances, and autograph parties, as we traveled all across Texas and to Miami, Memphis, and New York City. Meeting in private homes, public libraries and churches, speaking at colleges, women's groups, IBPOE Elks' and political conventions, we talked to Americans from all walks of life, eager to honor Mrs. Hunt and buy the book.

The book began to take on new forms. In August 1983, dramatic excerpts were included in a showcase production of Texas writers staged at the world-renowned White Barn Theatre in Westport, Connecticut. And in October 1987, Women and Their Work produced a musical version, "I Am Annie Mae," at St. Edward's University in Austin, Texas. The lyrics and music were composed by a Houston poet and educator, Naomi Carrier, and together we wrote the script for an ensemble production. The eight

Houston library

Houston Post

Houston

Houston Chronicle

x

performances played to sold-out houses and standing-room-only crowds. The enthusiasm propelled us to acceptance as the showcase of the Texas Playwrights Festival in Houston in June and July 1989 in a production by Stages Theatre. Since then, a one-woman version has traveled to dozens of college campuses and communities, delighting (and educating) audiences.

Members of black communities have rallied around Mrs. Hunt, not only as a symbol of one woman's strength and survival, but as a testament of community pride and achievement. On one emotion-packed Saturday afternoon in Houston's Johnson Branch Library, with all seats packed, including many Hunt grandchildren and "greats," one young woman was so moved by Mrs. Hunt's remarks that she wrote a poem while Mrs. Hunt was talking and read it, to the audience's delight. Ada Simond, an Austin historian, wrote, "*I Am Annie Mae* is priceless. I could not put it down. It might well have been the story of many of my aunts and uncles." Mrs. Hunt was given the keys to Austin, and designated a "Yellow Rose of Texas" by the Governor.

Book orders have come from both coasts and mid-America—from Harvard, Antioch, Princeton, Winston-Salem, Mt. Holyoke, Virginia Foundation for the Humanities, U.S. Army Corps of Engineers, Dallas Public Library, University of Texas, and Somerset, Texas, High School, among many. Professors use the book in courses of African American and Women's Studies, history, sociology, and literature. Excerpts have also been used in anthologies of black history and literature.

Mrs. Hunt sells the book to strangers as she travels on buses and planes. Wherever she goes, the book goes with her. Her children and grandchildren, with a new sense of their family history, have been her biggest boosters.

Oral history is an ongoing, opening-up process. It does not end with the publication of a book. Mrs. Hunt continues to remember incidents from her life and work. We can all relate to her because she is a real woman. Being real, her story is believable and touches us in familiar ways. It is warm and personal. It is like reading a diary.

Annie Mae Hunt hears advice from her "own self's mind," and she listens to it. Her inner wisdom has seen her family through hard times with their spirits intact. It has made her a self-styled "queen bee," the focus of a rich community life, a source of support and guidance for her neighbors, friends, children, and many grandchildren. It has taken her from picking cotton under near-slavery conditions, to housework, to sewing and selling Avon, to retirement in a home she owns, to active participation in politics and club work, and to attending a presidential inauguration.

This material represents the best promise of oral history—the ability to document the lives of ordinary working class people who are at the base of all political structures, but who are seldom included in the history books. Augmented by what she remembers of her grandmother's tales, and by events in the lives of her children and grandchildren, Mrs. Hunt's narrative covers a span of roughly 120 years in the history of black women in Texas. Her grandmother Matilda Boozie was a slave; her daughter Leona operates a computer.

Sociologist Rose Brewer has pointed out that there is no "prototypical" black Texas woman; but she observed that Mrs. Hunt's story personifies a wide range of the experiences of women of African descent in this state. There is a deep segmentation of the labor market along racial and gender as well as class lines; the lowest-paid tier of the Texas work force has always been occupied by black women. Today they are still overrepresented among domestic and service occupations, such as those performed

Annie Mae Hunt Day in Austin

Austin

Austin American-Statesman

Miami

Miami Herald

*NYC autograph party
Womanbooks*

*NYC National Council of
Negro Women, Women's
Center Workshop*

New York

by Mrs. Hunt, her mother, and her grandmother during much of their lives.

Yet Mrs. Hunt's story also illustrates a remarkable resistance to the vise of caste. After a life devoted to washing, cooking, ironing, picking cotton, and chopping cotton, she turned her back on domestic work and crossed over into the small business world of a self-employed woman. Her selling cosmetics and sewing are similar to other business niches occupied by black women who served the black community: beauty shop operators, milliners, funeral-home operators, café and boarding-house owners. Mrs. Hunt's grandmother's story touches on other economic roles as well. Matilda Boozie Randon was a respected and well-paid midwife, and she and her husband were among the relatively few black landowners who were able to hire other black workers for wages and as sharecroppers. *cf. Roarke, Black Masters*

Survival for black women has not been simply or solely a matter of making money to live on. It has also been the task of maximizing the scarce resources available to them and their families. Married three times, Mrs. Hunt nevertheless spent much of her life in the role of the single parent. To insure survival in times of hardship, she drew close with the women who lived around her, relying on their help and cooperation. When she says, "You don't need a *certain* someone, just someone who cares," she is expressing a lifeway and a philosophy of mutual aid among neighbors and friends.

In the face of segregation, the black community has developed strong institutions of its own, which are bases for activities of many women. Mrs. Hunt explains how the black Elks organization evolved separately from the white organization because of exclusion, and how the new organization added "Improved" to its title. Though Mrs. Hunt does not represent the elite of black club women, club work is of tremendous importance to her life also. She has a strong attachment to her church—particularly the church she attended as a child, which has an annual "homecoming."

Many injustices have been perpetrated on Annie Mae McDade Prosper Hunt: by her father, her employers, her situation, and society at large. Never resigned, always moving toward improvement, she has a philosophy of setting aside possible sources of bitterness. "That was the way of life," she says, summing up in a single phrase the blindness of the sinners and the acceptance of the sinned-against. "That was the way of life then."

As Curator of the Texas Foundation for Women's Resources History Project and traveling exhibition "Texas Women—A Celebration of History" and as author of *Black Texas Women: 150 Years of Trial and Triumph*, I have studied the lives of thousands of Texas women. They were brave, resourceful, creative, and strong, and I love them all. But I have yet to meet a woman I admire more than Annie Mae Hunt, and I have never heard a story more fascinating than the one she told me. This is her story.

—Ruthe Winegarten

Should "A Thousand Springs" find its way to a commercial production in New York, D.C., or any other important theater city, it would be all to the good if in that cast were several of those who brought the work to life at The White Barn. It would be hard to top Cynthia Dorn doing "Annie Mae Hunt," an oral history put together by Ruthe Winegarten in which Dorn gives chilling account of what it was like to be black in the Texas of 1922.

"A Thousand Springs"
White Barn Theatre
WESTPORT, CONNECTICUT

I am Annie Mae

"I Am Annie Mae" was produced as a musical for the first time in October, 1987, by Women and their Work in Austin, Texas, at St. Edward's University. The musical was written by Naomi Carrier (composer and lyricist) and Ruthe Winegarten and was directed by Boyd Vance.

Danna Byrom

Danna Byrom

Naomi Carrier
and Annie Mae Hunt

Tomas Pantin

I am Annie Mae Hunt.
I were born in 1909 in
Washington County on
Mill Creek Road.

Grandmother remembered very well the day they sold her mother 1 ≣≣≣≣≣≣

I am Annie Mae Hunt. My name now is Hunt. And my first three children don't want me to lose "Prosper," so I kept it. But really my name should be Annie Mae McDade. That's what I was born. That's my daddy's name, George McDade. Annie Mae McDade Prosper Hunt, that's what it really is.

I were born in 1909 in Washington County on Mill Creek Road, 13 miles out from Brenham near Wesley. I were reared there until I were eight, when my mother moved to Dallas. Five or six years later, it was Depression time and we moved to Navasota, on a plantation where we met a little tragedy. And from then on we went back to Brenham where my grandmother was.

c. 1922
an agricultural
depression

Well, when I were born, my grandmother was 60-something, 62, 63 years old. But she lived to be 101 years old. And she died in 1947 when I was pregnant with Othella. My grandmother was a very wonderful woman. She told me many a stories about herself and slavery. She was born in South Carolina [1] and her white people was Boozies, and I understand that some of them live there now, but she left there, and they came to Mt. Pleasant in Texas. When my grandma was moved down to Brenham, Texas, in Washington County, I know it was after slavery. Now I don't know how they got down in Washington County. I never could understand how they got there from Mt. Pleasant. [2] At that time it was a long way. But Washington

c. 1846–1849 ?

Titus County
1850s ?

I were born in Washington County on Mill Creek Road.

a slave cabin in
Mt. Pleasant,
Texas

*My grandmother was born
in South Carolina and her
white people was Boozies.
But she left there and they
came to Mt. Pleasant in
Texas.*

4

County[3] is where I were born, my mother and them was born and raised there, too.

My grandmother's name was Matilda, Matilda Boozie, cause her white people was Boozies, so she was a Boozie.[4] Cause when you were sold, you took whoever bought you, their name. Like, if George Washington bought you, then you were Annie Washington.[5] Her name was Matilda Boozie, but they called her Tildy.

My grandmother was known as a house girl. That means you worked in the house with Old Mistress and they liked you, you had more than anybody else . . . you had more than any of the other black slaves. There was another slave named Calvin, was her age. She always slipped him food and stuff.

My grandmother always said she remembered very well the day they sold her mother.[6] I don't know how old she was, but she was able to work, she was in the house with Old Mistress. And grandmother cried and cried, and Old Mistress hugged her and told her, "Don't worry, Tildy. I'll take care of you." And she did. She took care of her.

c. 1850s ?

"Don't worry, Tildy. I'll take care of you." That's all Grandma knew. She had sisters and a brother, and she never heard from them no more.[7] When I got to be a grown woman and had all these children, there was a lady lived down in Fayetteville, Texas, near where we were, who had the same name that Grandma had, come from the same place—South Carolina. It was my boyfriend's grandmother. And my grandmother and his grandmother looked just alike. But by them being old, it was hard for Grandma to go see about her. She always said, "I'm going down there and talk to Mrs. Dobb's mother." But she never did.

Fayette County

Fayette County Ordinance [8]

1862

Any male slave

about the age of 16 years

who may be found by the patrol on any night visit
to be absent from the premises of his master
without a lawful pass in writing shall be liable
to be punished *with not more than*

twenty-five lashes.

Preachers and paddy rollers — something to control the slaves 2

My grandmother say when she was growing up during slavery time, they had preachers. The white people would get black men that had a speech, that could talk. Some peoples are born with a speech. If you ain't got a speech when you're young, you don't have none no way.

Well, the white men would put those black men with a speech in a long-tailed coat, white shirt, and black tie, and tell them what to preach about. And those preachers would preach what the white man say they should: "Y'all gonna help old mawster do this and he gonna take care of you. The Bible tells you that in there."

If you run off, you was considered sick. The whites had a bunch of men then, something like the Ku Klux Klans. They called them *Paddy Rollers*, and they would catch you and whup you, and you was afraid. It was something to control the slaves.

Patrollers

They had to have something to control these people, and you wasn't allowed to go off the farm and visit other people. On certain days you had to have a pass. It was the way of life then.

Here's a picture of my first uncle Theodore Randon, the son of Young Mawster and my grandmother Matilda Boozie. They called him Nigger *but he's a white man.*

Tildy, who been messin wit you down there 3

I didn't know my first uncle, but I've always seen his picture, all my life. It's a lovely picture. They called him *Nigger* but he's a white man.[9] That's all he was. Old Young Mawster's son.

Grandma say that she were near 13 years old, behind the barn *tee-'teein* when Young Mawster come up behind her. She didn't see him, but he put his hand up under her dress, and said, "Lay down, Tildy." They called her Tildy, but her actual name was Matilda. And so this thing happened, and her stomach began to get big.

One day, Grandma and Old Mistress, they was puttin up the clean clothes. Old Mistress had a pair of socks, or two pair, in her hand. She said, "Tildy, who been messin wit you down there?" Grandma say, "Young Mawster." Old Mistress ran to her, and crammed these socks in her mouth and say, "Don't you never tell nobody. If you do, I'll skin you alive."

Tildy was already Old Mistress' favorite slave, so when his baby was born, she was certainly their favorite slave. Old Mistress were the grandmother of Tildy's baby. After Tildy was freed, they gave her this 1500 acres of land down there in Washington County, 14 miles out in the country, on account of this illegitimate baby that my grandmother had by this young mawster.[10]

c. 1859–1864 ?
urinating

c. 1860–1870s ?

9

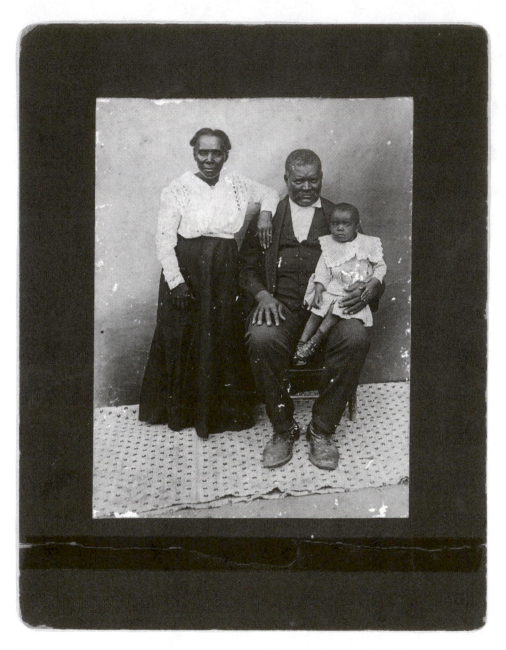

My grandparents, Matilda Boozie Randon and Eli Randon, holding my brother George around 1909. It was a beautiful marriage cause they lived together so long.

Grandmother say they would step over the broom 4

My grandpa's name was Eli Randon. I don't know how he and Grandma met. He spoke mighty little. I don't know if he met her from another farm or what. Or did he meet her after slavery? He always told me he was a Seminole Indian. He looked like it. Big tall guy. And my grandma was part Cherokee. [11] She had pretty hair.

And I learned after I were grown and had my children, that they never was married by a court. They didn't know any better. And when some of their children find out, they want them to get married. But then they said, "No, we're not going to bring the disgrace on my mama. They've been saying all this time they were married. Let them stay like they was." They was married like people did do in that time in Navasota. [12]

My grandmother, grandfather was married by the people that she was raised by. Grandmother say they would step over the broom and step back, and the preacher would say something, and she had on her old mistress' wedding dress. Old Mistress gave her that wedding dress. It was beautiful, Grandmother said. That was the way they were married, and they lived together till death did they part. [13] And it was a beautiful marriage cause they lived together so long.

And these people gave them 1500 acres of land when she . . . they married them on account of this illegitimate baby that my grandmother had by this young mawster . . . they gave them 1500 acres of land, and they lived there for years.

11

My mother, Callie Randon, was the baby, my grandmother's 16th child.

My mother had a beautiful childhood 5 ≡≡≡≡≡≡

My grandmother had 16 children, and she didn't

have any retarded children, either. Everybody was in their right mind, and that was beautiful. With that many children, usually somebody be crippled, but all of them was normal. My first uncle, old Young Mawster's son, Theodore Randon, is the onliest one that I never see, because he got killed.[14] But I've got his picture. I've got it today, settin back in my den.

1892–1893

My mother, Callie Randon, was the baby, my grandmother's 16th child. She grew up in Washington County, Brenham, Texas, out in the country. We never lived in town. Had a farm about two miles out of a little village called Wesley. After Mother got some size, they moved into a new house that Grandpa bought in Washington County, Wesley. They were all reared up and went to school down there.

b. 1889

c. 1900 ?
part of Wesley is in Washington County, part in Austin County

Mama went to school, but she didn't get no further than the fifth grade. She was lucky to get that far. I didn't get no further than the fifth grade either.

Well, my mother had a beautiful childhood. My grandaddy and them lived well. If anything happened to Mama, she'd always prefer to go home where Grandaddy was because he had money. I was one of his favorite grandchilds. I had everything I wanted when Grandaddy was living.

Grandpa had this 1500 acres of land what these white people gave them, on account of this illegitimate baby Grandmother had by this Young Mawster. Grandpa had houses on that land. He had people living on his place, and they worked

13

on halvers. When Grandpa had to furnish his mules and plows for you to work, I think that was halves. Sharecroppin. They done that kind of work. But some of these people, my grandfather's niece Pinky and her husband, lived on Grandpa's place, but they had their own mules and wagons, and came in different.[15]

Grandpa worked people by the week or by the month; he didn't work people all the time. I don't think he paid them much. It wasn't over 50 cents a day, cause that's all Mama and Uncle Julius and them was gettin, 50 cents a day. That was the way of life then.

He paid them as he went along. Used to pay in checks, little checks made in that part of the country. Worth maybe 25 cents. They were like money or food stamps. But they had to spend it at a certain place, I think Joe McKester's store.

similar to arrangements made by white land owners

Mikeska

This is the well that set on the porch of Joe McKester's store. That store—it ain't there any more—straddled the county line.

*February 23, 1877
Eli Randon buys 110 acres on Mill Creek in Austin County from J. H. and Lucy Davis for $2090, to be paid $418 down and in four promissory notes, 10% annual interest.

November 2, 1877
Eli Randon buys 108¾ acres from Andrew Herring for $1600 with eight deferred promissory notes of $200 each.

February 1, 1878
Eli Randon sells the 110 acres he had purchased from the Davises in 1877 to James Wilkins for $1850, $250 down and $1600 in a promissory note due in 1880 at 12% annual interest.

August 1, 1883
Eli and Matilda Randon buy 43 acres in Washington County from Henry and Green May for $1. (The Mays may have had trouble making payments. Original sale to the Mays was not found.)

February 15, 1907
Eli Randon buys two lots in Brenham for $100.

September 12, 1916
Eli and Matilda Randon sell the Brenham lots for $170.

Deed No. 274

J. H. Davis & wife
to
Eli Randon — Deed

The State of Texas
County of Austin

Know all men by these presents that we Joshua Davis and Lucy E. Davis husband and wife of State and County aforesaid for and in consideration of the sum of Two Thousand and ninety ($2090.00) Dollars gold to be paid by "Eli" Randon also of said as follows towit: four hundred and eighteen dollars gold to be paid one day date, four hundred and eighteen gold dollars to be paid on the first day January A.D. 1878, four hundred and eighteen dollars gold to be paid on the first day of January A.D. 1879 four hundred and eighteen dollars to be on the first day of January A.D. 1880, and four hundred and eighteen dollar gold to be paid on the first day of January A.D. 1881, and to secure the payment of said sums of money on the dates as aforesaid the said "Eli" Randon has executed and delivered to us his certain five (5) promisory notes bearing even herewith all of said notes are payable to the order of the said Joshua H. Davis with interest at the rate of ten per cent per annum from this date, and hold and carry the Vendors lien on the hereinafter described tract or parcel of have granted bargained sold released and conveyed and by these presents do grant bargain sell release and convey unto the said "Eli" Randon his heirs and assigns all the following described tract or parcel of land lying and being situate in the forks of Mill Creek in said County of Austin it being a part of the Eaton League and more fully described as follows towit: beginning at a rock set for Mrs. Sanders NW corner Thence N. 43 E. with Mrs. Sanders line 1201 vrs. to Bidy branch; Thence N. 47 W. at 514 vrs. set a stake in field Thence S. 43 W. 1201 vrs. to a rock for Willies corner Thence S. 47 E. with Willies line 574 vrs. to the place of beginning Containing 110 acres of land, together with all and singular the rights members hereditaments and appurtenances to the same belonging or in any wise incident or appertaining To have and to hold all and singular the said premises unto him the said "Eli" Randon his heirs and assigns in fee simple forever. and we the said Joshua H. Davis and Lucy E. Davis do hereby bind ourselves our heirs executors and administrators to warrant and forever defend all and singular the said premises unto him the said "Eli" Randon against the claims of any and all persons lawfully claiming or to claim the same or any part thereof. In testimony whereof we hereunto sign our names — scrolls for seals as of the 23d day of February A.D. 1877

J. H. Davis (seal)
Lucy E. Davis (seal)

They lived on that 1500 acres of land for years. It was a beautiful place. I don't know how it was, but Grandpa lost all that as time went by. I always meant to dig into it. Times was hard, I guess. He finally got rid of some of this land, sold this, sold that. Just didn't know any better what to do. But he shouldn't ever have gotten rid of all he did, because after he got rid of it, the oil field came there.[16] It's there now. Washington County. As time went by, Mama moved down close to the Brenham oil field where she could work on a job down there. She cooked for the oil people.

My grandparents bought another place, a few hundred acres, when I was four years old. I remember the very day that we moved to this place. It was a beautiful place.[17]

1912–1915

Wesley

1913

They lived on that 1500 acres of land for years. It was a beautiful place.

My grandmother caught
everybody in that country,
white or black. She
was good and she was
recognized.

Grandma was a midwife 6 ====

My grandmother was a midwife. Every white man or black man born in that country that's my age, my grandma *caught* him. They called it *catch em*. Yes, a many a one down there right today.[18]

Grandma would go and stay three and four weeks with a family, according to how rich they was. The Hodes, the Yah-nishes, the Wobblers, they all were rich people, Bohemian, German, Polish people. Yeah, that's what that country's made out of.

She was woke up many a night, and stayed right there with that woman until she got up. There wasn't nothing they could do for pain. Grandma kept quinine. Now they had a doctor in there, was a doctor named Kanale, and one that name Wooskie. They'd give them quinine. They knew just how much to give them. Now what that quinine was for, I don't know.

And Grandma had another little medicine in a bottle, real dark red. I don't know what it was. Grandma kept also a black bag, just like a doctor did, she kept it. And we wasn't allowed to touch it. We couldn't even look at it too hard, cause every-thing she needed was there. She had her scissors and her thread that she cut the baby's cord, and she had it right there. Where the doctors tie the baby's cord now with certain plastic and catguts and stuff, Grandma had big number eight white spools of thread, and she kept it in this bag.

In those days quinine was used as an all-purpose medicine. It is also a drug commonly used to bring on an abortion.

possibly mercurochrome, a very old medicine

Everybody paid her—except sometimes the colored people didn't. It wasn't no more than three dollars to *catch* a baby. She stayed with the rich white people, doing their washing and ironing, and taking care of the woman's baby and her chores. Those Polish and German people had a hell of a chore. Those women worked like dogs. They'd do anything a man would do, go out and plow. Now the rich women didn't do this, but the rich white woman's daughter got out and plowed like her brother did. And when the mamas didn't have no small babies, they worked in the fields too. Grandma didn't do that; she'd wash and iron.

And when Grandma came home, they would give her 25, 30 dollars, and that was a whole lot of money. She'd have everything she needed, all kinds of clothes and meat, and she'd bring light bread home, and we was there to gobble it up cause we loved it.[19]

She *caught* everybody in that country, white or black. You better know she did. She had a name for herself. She was good and she was recognized!

"rich" is relative

21

OCT · 55

The church has always been important in my family. My grandpa was a Baptist preacher. This is my cousin, the Reverend Charles Randon, Assistant Pastor of the True Light Baptist Church in Dallas.

Grandpa was a hypocritin Baptist preacher 7

I always said my grandfather was a hypocritin Baptist
preacher. Grandma say he would leave home in January
when they turn over the land for the snow and ice to kill the
bugs, and when he come back, they'd be done picked their
first bale of cotton. That was the way. He would always leave
before they turned over the land, and get back in time to sell
the first bale.

His children did all his work, and then the grandchildren.
There were David and my baby uncle Eli.[20] There was Les,
one of Grandma's niece's child. Grandma's niece Sylvia was
her age, but she had children, and raised those children out
there.

Grandma and them raised me till I were eight years old,
until we moved to Dallas. And I'd go back to their farm every
year after school was out. We picked peanuts, we picked peas,
we chopped cotton. Grandpa had a truck patch; he would sell
this stuff—peas and peanuts and watermelons—biggest I've
ever seen in my life.

It was a happy life with them. When the end of school
come, no sooner we'd get down there, we found ourself doing
this work on Dogwood Creek, that's where the beautiful dogwood trees bloom every year. And I loved every inch of the
ground where they lived.

1917

runs from
Washington
County into
Austin County

23

And when people would work for Grandpa and them, they come by going home, and my Grandma would sell milk. It was either a dime or a nickel a gallon.

They had milk all around them 8 ≣≣≣

My grandaddy and grandmother had a house.

Precious house, I called it—very precious to me—and it only
had three rooms. This is the house they built when I was four
years old, four or five miles out from Wesley in Austin County.
And they built a kitchen on the outside of this house, and the
kitchen had three rooms. Attic over where the stove was—a
big wood stove, and it had a dirt floor, had a box where you put
your wood. Over here was a great big dining room. And then
the other part was a kitchen where we'd eat, there wasn't
nobody but us. In the morning early, we'd come out in the
kitchen and eat right here. Our farm joined Grandpa's farm,
and their house was close enough for us to walk. That was
Grandma's precious kitchen and I loved it.

    The kitchen was behind the house, and it had some big
trees in the yard behind, and on these trees had big boxes
nailed up with screens around them where they put their milk,
and this would keep the flies and things off. No refrigerators.
Grandma let her butter down in the well a many day. And
she had something like a cupboard that set against the wall in
this part of the kitchen where we all ate. It was a great big
thing where she kept other milk in great big milk cans. They
had milk all around them. And when people would work for
Grandpa and them, they come by going home, and my
Grandma would sell milk. It was either a dime or a nickel a
gallon. She would sell them sausage. Cut one of them sau-

1913

A sketch would be handy

25

My grandma and grandpa, Matilda Boozie Randon and the Rev. Eli Randon. My grandmother was a wonderful woman. She told me many a stories about herself and slavery.

sages down. Anything they want. Grandmother and them never would see any money for this. It was taken off those workers' salary. Grandpa worked them by the week or by the month. He paid them as he went along. I just wonder sometimes what kind of wages would they have when they get through, but I wasn't big enough to remember any of that.

*I got my grandma's lamp
here. Oil went down in
there. But I broke the
globe.*

Indoor plumbing? Are you kidding? 9

As time went on, a lot of rich people began to get
Delco lights[21] in their houses. They had little sheds built, that
motor going all the time. We never had anything like that. My
grandpa could have had electricity, cause he had money to do
it, but he never did want it. You just didn't want things then like
you do now. You wasn't used to it.

We used lamps. I got my grandma's lamp here. Oil went
down in there. You had to clean it from time to time. My
grandma had certain times that she would clean everything.
When she'd get through washing, she'd have lye in the pot,
and she said, "Get that lamp out of there, y'all, and wash those
globes." We'd put rocks and soap suds in those lamps, and
shake em and really clean em. We'd wet the rag in ashes and
wash them. They'd clear up so pretty. Now we got Ajax, but
ashes done the same thing. And sand will do the same thing
right now.

Grandma and Grandpa didn't have no indoor water; they
had wells out in the yard. They had a bucket on each end of a
rope, and they would put one down and draw this bucket up,
and this other bucket went down. As time went by, they got
a little modern with different types of buckets that wouldn't
break. When the bucket hit the water, it would fill up through a
hole in the bottom, and when you'd draw it up, a plug would
sink down in the bottom. They were gettin modern then.

Indoor plumbing? Are you kidding? My grandpa and

29

them, we never had a toilet until I was grown and had children out there. We went out in the woods. No, we didn't have an outhouse either. But as time went by, I guess Grandpa and them got old and couldn't stoop down no more like they used to. Then they had an outhouse built, a big hole, and you put something down in it to eat up the stuff, and you didn't have to take it up no more.

This looks just like my mama when she lived in West Texas. Look like Mama washin with the pots around the trees.

Grandma didn't believe in no-dingy clothes

10

I remember when there wasn't no washing powder.
We used soap. When washing powder first came out, it came in barrels. Talk about that, most everything came in barrels. First washing powder I remember my mama using here in town was the Gold Dust Twins. But after that, we'd go and buy washing powder by the pound in sacks. Bon Ami—that was one of the early Ajaxes and Comets, and also we had this little hard soap thing. It was white, and it was rough. When you got ready to wet your rag, you put that in, and you scrubbed. I can see it now.

c. 1917

you mean, you didn't?

    I remember my grandma and them washin. They had wash basins side the smoke houses. We had more than one smoke house, too, a smoke house where she hung her meat and stuff, and one where she put her kraut and her preserves. They put all that stuff up.

preserve

    And one of those smoke houses always had a line of benches, and my grandma would wash, have six or seven tubs of water there. I remember the time Grandma's well went dry, and we had to tote the tubs of water from the spring fore we went to work. She always had lots of *rinch* waters. This first *rinch* water wasn't good enough, she'd wash with the third *rinch water*. Always *rinchin*. And my grandma had a wash *pit* there. She used lye. She put them clothes in that lye water. Boiled them clothes like boilin beans. Boil them clothes, juice em down like that, and wash them clothes. Grandma had

rinse
rinsing
shed where the pots were housed

31

pretty white clothes. You didn't see nothin dingy in her house till they got to be rags. A whole lot of times, today, they got polyester, it just turns dingy. But a long time ago, they had pure cotton, and Grandma's clothes didn't get dingy like you see some people's clothes. She didn't believe in no dingy clothes.

My mother had a beautiful childhood. My grandaddy and them lived well. Yeah, they always lived well. And when Mama was a baby, Grandaddy, he'd give anything to Mama.

My mother Callie Randon McDade.

My father George McDade.
Here he is at the age of 17
in his first pair of long
pants. About 1901.

My daddy
Stole
my mama 11 ≡≡≡≡≡≡≡≡≡

My mother's name was Callie Randon, and my father
was George McDade, and my brother had the same name. He
was a junior. George McDade, Jr.

My mother met my daddy, George McDade, and he *stole*
my mama. They call it *elope* now. But at that time Grandma
say he *stole* her. She was about 16 years old. My grandma
looked for my daddy and her for three weeks in a wagon with
a shotgun laying across her lap. Grandmother was going to
shoot him if she found him. And always in our house there
was a joke about Grandmother looking for Daddy with a shotgun across her lap. She was going to shoot him for *stealing*
her baby. Yeah, she was mad, but she got over it.

c. 1905

*My mama worked like a
dog. Pick cotton. Chop
cotton. That's all she knew.*

Wash, cook and iron. Pick cotton. Chop cotton. 12 ≡

My mama had three children. There was George, the oldest, Annie Mae, that's me, and Dora, the baby. Mama were 20 when I were born.

George, b. 1907
Annie, Mae, b. 1909
Dora, b. 1911
1916

My daddy left Mama when I was seven years old. My daddy didn't hardly know I was alive, we were alive, until we got just about grown. And Mama had to support the family. And she did. She worked like a dog. She didn't know anything but working hard in a house as cook, wash and iron; that's all she know to do. Wash, cook and iron. Pick cotton, chop cotton. That's all she knew.

Mama had moved up to Wesley, and then we were all born, but then she moved down close to that oil field where she could work. Mama worked on the oil field in Washington County where she was raised, cookin on a job down there. She cooked for the oil people.

c. 1913–1917

When I were eight, she came here to Dallas. She managed. Me and my sister, she put us on a row together, chopped cotton right here in the Dallas area. In Mesquite. Put us on a little row together. We *made a day*, two people *made a day*. That's right. And it was 50¢ a day. A lot of people worked for 50¢ a day. I mean this is when I was a girl, and I'm 68 years old now. And I remember when cotton choppin went up—this man give a dollar a day.

1917

the equivalent of a day's work

I was lucky to get to the fifth grade, because we had to work. Every time school was out for the summer, we'd

37

go back to Grandma's, and we wouldn't get back to Dallas till October. I've gone to school since I've been grown—went over here at Frazier on Spring Avenue and learnt. Course I know how to read and write. There's a lot of things I can execute, but I'm not a good talker. I speak sometimes in church, but I put it on paper first. But if you ask me a question, then I can answer that.

When we first moved to Dallas, we were young and we enjoyed it. We didn't want to be out in the sun working; yet we were eager to leave here when school was out, ready to go where Grandma and Grandpa was. They weren't too hard on us, making us work, till we got to be a pretty good size.

The best job Mama ever had was with some people named Fogler. They had a big farm, and we lived on their place, and Mrs. Fogler would have Mama to help her fix meals for the people that worked for them, and they would feed us. Mother worked for these people and cooked for the hands, and they would feed us, and they would also give us clothes, and I never had a hard time that I knew anything about it.

When things would get sort of bad, Grandpa would always step in. I didn't know that until I was older. My mama told me that cause I knew, we was up here in Dallas one time, and Grandpa came all the way up here. At the time I didn't know what he was doing, but I got older and learnt he was paying rent and buying us food. When Grandpa left, we had a 100 pound sack of sugar, had flour, two 48-pound sacks. We had rice. Cause that's the way my grandpa bought groceries. See, they harvest their crops in the fall of the year, and then they buy their food, coffee and sugar and stuff.

And Grandpa and them always had hogs. It was a natural thing for him to bring us meat, cause he killed this meat and cured it, and bring us sausage and lard. As I said, we were

c. 1920–21

having a hard time, that's why Grandpa came with all that
sugar and stuff, and boy, we were living happy. Mama didn't
ever have to live hard, but Mama didn't want Grandpa and
them to take care of her. Like I wouldn't want my parents to
take care of me. So this is what happened.

*This dance hall was for
whites only. Now my
brother George used to
earn a little extra change by
cleaning it up.*

Greater People Baptist Church
1300 Bonnieview Rd.
Rev. A.A. McKnight, Pastor

Senior Choir

Presents

Mrs. Annie Mae Prosper Hunt

in

A Gospel And Spiritual Recital

Programme

```
Congregational Hymn
Mistress of Ceremonies...Mrs. Grace Washingto
Scripture ...............Rev. Norris Hamilton
Prayer...................Rev. J.L. Tennesion
Congregational Song......"What A Fellowship"
Welcome..................Mrs. Louise Richard
Respond..................Visitor
Presentation of Soloist..Mrs. E. Jewel Hamle
    1. A. - Give Me A Voice To Sing
       B. - I Trust In God
       C. - Step By Step
       D. - Let God Abide
    2. Guest Artists....Mrs. Jewel Morris
    3. A. - Thats Alright
       B. - All The Way
    4. Invitation.......Pastor McKnight
       Offering........Bro. R. Sparks,
                             W. Washington
    5. A. - Walk Around Hevan Allday
       B. - Close To Thee
       C. - How Great Thou Art
       D. - Twelve Gates To The City
    6. Presentation of Gifts
Acknowledgement of Visitors..Mrs. V. Powell
Remarks..................President Dunlap
```

*I still sing. I still gives
musicals. My voice have
gotten real deep now. I still
sings enough for people to
enjoy it.*

Miss Mattie, Annie's cryin cause her shoes hurt 13 ≣≣≣

Walkin wasn't nothing. Right here, Frances Dirks is
53 years old, she walked from right here in South Dallas to
Booker T. Washington High School over there in North Dallas.
I walked from Scott and Sunday up here to Taylor Street.
Every child out here walked. And as I say, the average white
person wasn't used to this kind of stuff.

1940s
About 5 miles.
There were at
least two white
(segregated) high
schools closer to
Frances's home.

c. 1915–1917

In Washington County, I started school fore I was six years
old. And small as I was, I walked for two years, I walked seven
miles to school every morning and thought nothing of it.
Seven miles every morning. Yeah, we always walked, believe it
or not. We didn't get too far to walk when I was a child. I
walked it for two years, and I left that country when I was eight
years old.

Oh, there was gobs of us. At that time, the country was
thick with black people, and they come from everywhere. In
the evening when we turn off, the road coming to four points,
some would go this way, some go that way, some go cross the
fields. Yeah, that's the way it was.

Once my daddy came up there just for the school closing.
We had good school closings, you see. People loved their
school. And of course I could sing, and my brother and sister
could sing. At these school closings in the spring, the teacher
always wanted the best, and me and my sister was always the
height of the show, cause we were singing. We had guts.

One time my daddy came and bought me some shoes
for the school closing, and came to hear us sing. And one of

This is where the New
School used to stand.
Those trees—the boys
used them for bases when
they played ball.

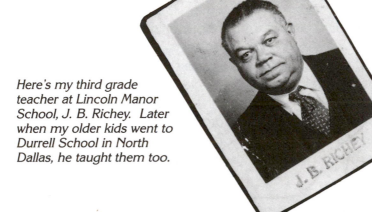

J. B. RICHEY

Here's my third grade
teacher at Lincoln Manor
School, J. B. Richey. Later
when my older kids went to
Durrell School in North
Dallas, he taught them too.

my teachers which I remember very well and loved was Mattie Fitch, my daddy's cousin. So when it was ready for me to go on and sing, I was cryin, so another cousin of mine said to Mattie Fitch, "Miss Mattie, Annie's cryin cause her shoes hurt."

Now whatever they put on our feet, we wore. And my shoes hurt, and I was cryin. Miss Mattie said, "Annie, what's the matter? Your feet hurting you?" She pulled off my shoes. And there I was singing. I had on a pair of those white ribbed stockings, real cotton ribbed stockings that they wore a long time ago, and a white ribbon, and I was standing there singing in my bare feet.

This was when the first World War was going on. Mama's sister's children had gone into the Army.[22] And one of Mama's brothers in Wellington, Texas, had two boys in, and then my uncle Eli, Mama's baby brother, he was in the Army. I was singing all those World War I songs: "Over there, over there"; "Somebody keep the home fires burning while your heart's a-yearning"; "Though the boys are far away, they'll come home some day." I really sang that night, but I was bare-feeted. My daddy couldn't take it.

My daddy got mad, and ask why did his child got to come out on stage bare-feeted. He had no right to get mad. Mama should have gotten mad, you know. If anybody was going to get mad, he wasn't the one who should have gotten mad. But he got mad. He bought those shoes. You see, I should have been consulted. But he didn't know about this at that time. They should have been very careful what they put on my feet, but that time they measured feet with a string and whatever they brought back you wore, you didn't say nothing, children didn't say nothing. It was just the way of life.

paternal authority

This is me. My mama told me about menstruating, what to expect.

Oh, mama, don't tell nobody that! 14

Yeah, my mama told me about menstruating, what

to expect. She said that she *came around*—that's what they called it, you know—*came around monthly*, when she was 10 years old, so "I'm going to tell you now cause you may do it." Told me how to protect myself, and sure enough I did. Three days before I was 11 years old, I started to menstruate. And she done already told me what to do.

1920

I wasn't afraid, like some girls were. I had a cousin that almost had hysterics. She thought some boy had something to do with her, and she knew no boy had had something to do with her. But she was bleeding, and she couldn't imagine what happened. She didn't know what was going on. She was all confused, and then her mama told her afterwards. She said she sure was glad to get that message that her mama give her late.

Well, we didn't have Kotex. Oh, no, no. I was telling my children about this, and they said, "Oh, Mama, don't tell nobody that." We took all soft rags and we used them, and when we got through using them, we put them up where nobody . . . this was a sacred thing, this was sacred. We put them in a bag or a sack and hid them, and then time you got out by yourself, you washed your rags out. When Grandma and them got through with their things, and when I was grown, when I got through with all my other washings, I'd make a little pile and I'd boil out my rags—we called them *rags*. And then you wouldn't hang them on the fence, you put them down on the grass

47

where people wouldn't see them. When they got dry, you picked them up and put them in a certain place until you used them next time. My children said, "Mama, you don't mean to tell me you done. . ." I says, "Honey, that was the way of life. That was just the way of life."

My stepdaddy seen two cars drive up with five mens. He decided he wasn't going to take no whuppin. He don't know how he got across that Brazos River. But he crossed that Brazos River.

We met a little tragedy on a Navasota plantation 15

Five or six years after Mama moved to Dallas—she were married again, must have been about 1922—it was Depression time[23]—and we moved down to Navasota, on a plantation in Grimes County, where we met a little tragedy. Navasota, Grimes County, was just across the river from Brenham, Washington County. And Washington County was a free *unclear* country, and Grimes County was slavery—well, that's what they say. Well, it was like slavery times, it was, it was. I worked in the fields down there. This old man had a big bell, and they rang the bell for them to unhook the mules and come to dinner, ring the bell for them to go back out at 1 o'clock; you know, that kind of stuff.

We had been back about seven or eight months, maybe not that long, when my stepdaddy Wilson said something out of line that wasn't for black people to say in that time. I never knew exactly what he said. Anyway, that evening when my stepdaddy put his mules up, Old Man Kirk, the overseer, he's dead now, called to him and said, "Now, Wilson, I know you didn't know what you were saying, but they're gonna come out here tonight and whup you up." He told my stepdaddy not to stay home that night. So my stepdaddy decided he wasn't going to take no whuppin. He laid down in the branch, and he say he seen two cars drive up with five mens, three mens driving in one car, two in another, and when he seen those mens drive by the house, he went berserk, he went half nuts. He was tween the house and the Brazos River. Went that way

49

*And you know, Old Man
Morrett whipped my mama,
and Bud Jones holdin her.
She couldn't walk for 13
weeks.*

to the Brazos River. He knew where people left their boats, but he say he don't even remember getting there. He don't know how he got across that Brazos River. But he crossed that Brazos River.

Those white people come in our house, and they pushed my mama around, pushed her up against the wall; told her she better get that *nigger* back, and of course we were standing there trembling, me and my brother and sister, just like little leaves on the tree when the wind's going through it. When they left, my mama decided then she couldn't stay there, she was leavin. Sent my brother to Brenham, and Grandpa sent us some fare. So we got ready one day, and went to town, so we could catch that train going down to Hempstead from Navasota.

Navasota
Brenham
Hempstead

It run about 2 or 3 or 4 o'clock in the morning. We were sitting there at Miss Sissy's house, laughing and talking, play-ing, the children. About 10:30 or 11 o'clock at night, here come Mr. Bud Jones[24] and told my mama, "Come on out here." She said, "I'm not going out there." And, of course, we all stood still when Mama spoke up, cause that's the only thing we had was Mama. He grabbed her, and pushed her out the door and off the porch, and she stumbled. And he pushed her on out the gate, an old gate, and when she got to the car, Old Man Morrett, he hauled off and slapped her three or four times, and throwed her in the front seat of the car. Then, at that time, we come running, me and my sister. My brother was gone. We jumped in the back seat, and they had her in the front seat with them, and slapped her and asked her questions all the way to the Navasota River near the farm, going on back down toward our house.

And you know, Old Man Morrett whipped her, and Bud Jones holding her. My mama couldn't walk for 13 weeks. And they broke my arm. This old guy, this overseer Mr. Kirk, told Mama there was no doubt, it was broke. I had to hold my arm in a sling like this two or three times a day, and then

Mama'd change it, and it come down. Then I'd put it back up, then back down, so it wouldn't grow stiff. I have trouble with it now, always have. I understand that where you been broke once, arthritis is fall in those places. And Old Man Morrett broke my sister's nose with a pistol. Mama had to take paper and tear it up, and put it up her nose so the wind could go through it, and it could heal up. By being broken here and knocked apart, by them keeping it pressed open, it made it grow funny. I'm sorry I'm crying. That was the way. That is what happened long time ago. [25]

rather hard to tell
what's going on
here + why? fn
doesn't help
much

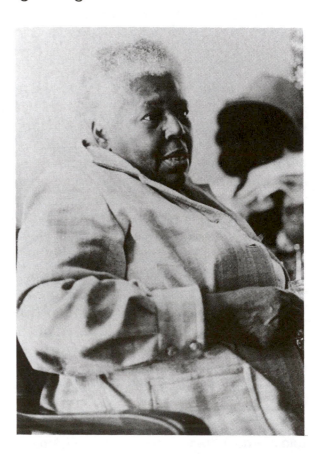

I don't take nothin off white folks either 16

I got married in 1924 to John Robert Prosper, and my mama finally left Navasota. You know, when times got bad down there, these people—the good Negroes, they called them—they all gone cotton pickin and have money when they came back. I mean, the boss had to feed them all year, and so he let them go on cotton pickin and things; and my mama promised him that she was going to come back. But Mama told Miss Sally, "You ever see me again, you'll have to come where I am." She told me one day, "I'll never come back here."

On her way out, Mama brought me her machine—a regular sewing machine something like this one here. You know, Old Man Morrett tried to get that machine. He come down and told my husband one day, "I want that machine that Callie brought up here." My husband was very quick-tempered. He says, "No, you can't get that machine." So the old man told my husband he didn't take nothing off our *niggers*, and my husband said, "I don't take nothing off white folks either." My husband was real high-tempered.

And so we were so afraid that this white man Morrett was going to come out there and do something to my husband, but my husband went around and told Mr. Steve Moore about it. My husband worked for this white man named Steve Moore, and Morrett didn't bother Steve Moore. Steve Moore must have had some kind of words to say about it, because

1927

53

that Old Man Morrett never tried to say anything about this machine no more.

That was a terrible time. There was this old woman up there in Navasota, Aunt Mehalia Jackson—I married in her family after this happened. And she had wanted to tell Mama she knew these white men were going to come for her, but she had to live there, and she didn't know what Mama may say. Aunt Mehalia couldn't afford to say nothing. They may whip Mama, and make Mama say who told.

Later my sister Dora married, and this Old Man Morrett came at my sister one time and took her off and kept her five or six hours. He had sex with her, raped her. That's all it was, because she wasn't willing. Oh, my sister like to went into hysterics. She never did get over that. It makes me cry to think about it. Sad, sad.

Now Dora had a husband at that time, Buck. Buck was Miss Two-T's brother. And Old Man Morrett come to their house one night, sent Bud Jones in after Buck. Two-T's mama said they were eating supper, and old Bud Jones come in and asked for Buck, and picked up Buck, and Buck ain't been seen since. They never did know what happened to Buck. That kind of stuff. My sister never got married again. That's the truth. This can be verified, what I'm telling you now can be verified. It's people living knows this—Buck's mother's dead, but his stepdaddy's still livin.

Old Man Morrett, he liked to rape black women. He went with Miss Joanna, Bud Jones' wife, and Bud knew it. Morrett made Bud leave home, so he could go to bed with Bud's wife. Miss Joanna got pregnant, and she told my mama, say she didn't know if the baby was going to be white or black.

I was prejudiced towards men 17

After this little tragedy in Navasota, well, I quit school and got married. I married very young, when I was 15. My husband was a farm boy. John Robert Prosper. His daddy was a sick man, and he had to work. Me and him had three children: Esther Mae Prosper, our oldest daughter, Dorothy Lou Prosper, and Doris Minola Prosper. And then we separated, and I went to live with my daddy in Houston, and he stayed down there and got married and had 12 more children.

Now my husband was a good man. I didn't know how to live with him. John Robert Prosper. I regretted it many a day that I couldn't live with him. But I didn't know how. I had so much prejudice in my heart, I didn't know how. I just didn't like what was going on. Well, he was going with another woman, and I knew it. I said to him, "I hear Sister ———— is pregnant. Is it yours?" He said, "Might be." That's what made me upset. I don't know if he was trying to be honest or just ornery. But he didn't say, "I'm sorry." He could have said, "No," even if it was. He didn't say that. Said, "It could be."

He was about the meanest man; he was mean; he was a mean man. If I'd had any sense I'd have stayed with him, with all them children. I wouldn't have taken on the burden of raisin all them children. That was hard. If you marry somebody else, you get the same thing. I just didn't know how to face my burden, so I left. That's the only thing I knew to do, so that's what I done. I left my children with my husband. I left during cotton pickin time too. I had a sack on my shoulder

why?

1924

Esther, b. 1925
Dorothy, b. 1928
Doris, b. 1930

c. 1932–1933

55

fn. is obscure

and I put my clothes in this sack, and the next year I went back and got the children.

See, I was prejudiced towards men. And here it is: I couldn't stand nothing a man do to me. My husband would hit me—I'd jump on him and claw his eyes, make me a scratch across his face.[26] I was prejudiced towards men. My daddy made me so. He used to beat my mama for everything she could think of. The only thing I wanted to do was tell my daddy how I felt. And I told my daddy before he died.

You know, he loved me more after that, more and more, cause I told him just what I thought about him. This was after I left my husband. I was asking my daddy for money. I had done a little ugly thing in Houston. I had hit a boy with a knife pretty hard, and the boy slapped me, and had called me an ugly name. I said, "Lord, he don't know what he is doing." And so I asked my daddy for money. I wanted to leave. I said, "The police are going to be after me. This boy have me arrested." My daddy said, "What?" He was very embarrassed. He wanted to know why. And I told him why.

So he gave me the money, and I went to Granger. I felt I could get refuge there. Ever since then, me and my daddy got along good. He asked me how long I been wanting to tell him that. I said, "I been wanting to tell you this all my life"—how ugly he was, how he did my mama. Mama'd fight him if she could. She'd whip him, but he wouldn't give her no chance; he would just leave. You know, we got some mean people today. I seen it on TV that wives, a man is beating them up. I tell you, a man never beat me up and got away with it!

Here I am with my baby
uncle Eli.

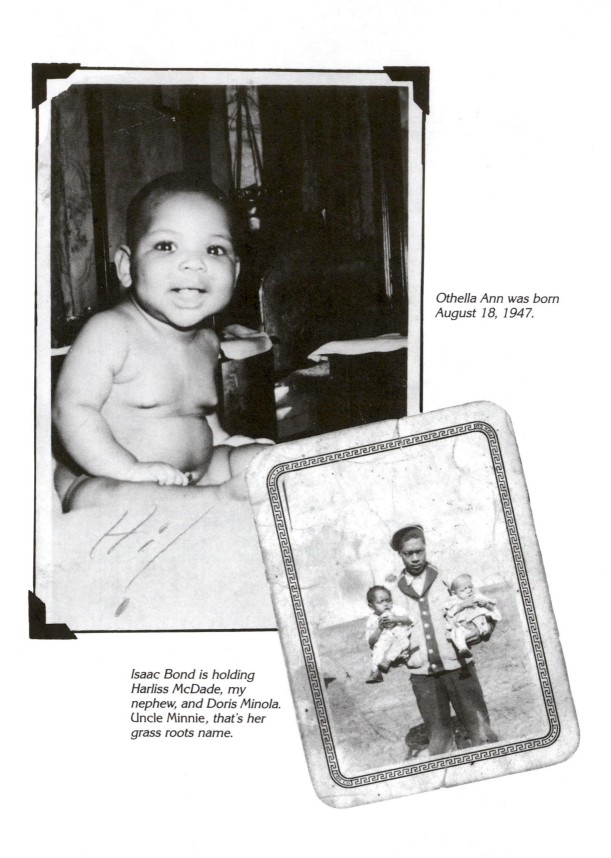

Othella Ann was born August 18, 1947.

Isaac Bond is holding Harliss McDade, my nephew, and Doris Minola. Uncle Minnie, that's her grass roots name.

I had my first baby
at fifteen and my last
at forty five 18

I was pregnant 13 times in all, and now I have six
children. I had my first baby, Esther Mae, when I was almost   1925
16, and my last one, Leona Louise, when I was 45. I was   1953
going to be 16 the 29th of August, and Esther was born on the
18th. About two years till I had the second child, Dorothy   1928
Lou. And I had a child which I lost between Dorothy Lou and   1929
the next one, Doris Minola. Miss Glann, a midwife in Navasota,   1930
delivered all three.

I lost three kids. Two of them died at birth, the other lived
to be two months. Having him, birthin him, was hard enough,
and then a child lives to be two months old. That's hard. I
woke up one morning about three o'clock and he was dead,
stiff dead, strangled to death.

I miscarried four times; they didn't get to be babies.
Some of the pregnancies was only three or four months. I
gave birth to nine children. Six are still alive. Pregnant 13
times, that's hard on a woman, too. You don't realize it.

I nursed all my babies except my last two. My little boy,
George, my fourth baby, was born in 1941. George was delivered by the doctors from Baylor Hospital. They came to my
home. Well, they done that all the time. The pregnant women
went to the clinic, and the doctors knew just about what time
you were going to deliver. They had you on the agenda, waitin
for you. Sometime they'd be with one woman, leave that one,
go to another one. That's what they used to do. Everything
was getting pretty modern then, but I nursed George. He was

59

a big little boy, and he would say, "Come on, Mama, let's go home. I want some tit." That's what he used to tell me. He was just one year old.

He's the only one I had, seven months old, could talk like a natural man. You know, say words: "bread"; we had some twins across the street, Dorothy and Doris, and he'd say, "two Doris." "Mama," "Papa," "bread," said as plain as day. He was as smart as a whip. Always been smart. He's smart right today.

His name is George Washington Darden. Born January 14, 1941. And Othella Ann Hunt, she was born August 18, 1947. And then Leona Louise Hunt, she were born November 19, 1953. And that's it. She's my baby now.

George (Sonny) and Othella

I wrote this in the middle of the night.

OUR OWN DAUGHTER, LITTLE RUBY JOYCE

1.

She were born in to the world
Those she never open her eyes
But we love her so much
Our own Daughter little Ruby Joyce

2

Daddy an I will never forget you
Altho it's so hard to fear
But we will try to meet our darling
Little Ruby Joyce over there

3.

Dear lord, we want you to help us
An to stand by us each day
So we'll be able to meet her
Our own Daughter little Ruby Joyce

4.

Mother an Daddy will always love you
Just long as we live in this world
An in that great Judgement Morning
We'll meet our own Daughter little Ruby Joyce

George and Othella at a birthday party in 1950

They called it *throwing away* <u>babies</u> 19

Oh, abortions, are you kidding? When I got to be a young woman, the women began to—they called it *throwing away babies*. So-and-so, that woman *throwed away* three babies. They would do things to theirself. That's why so many women died.

So many of our colored women died, because their mamas would do it themselves. And they would do a whole lot of silly things. I never did try that. I always was afraid. I was a God-fearing person. I didn't believe in doing things to me if I didn't know what I was doing, and I wasn't going to let you do it. I had an aunt one time, that's what she wanted to do to me. I said, "No, I don't believe in that." Well, O.K., I don't want these babies, but I got them, and I'm not going to do anything. You ain't gonna kill me.

Girls would do so many silly things. They would take things, and open theirselves up, go up in theirselves. Take bluing, and put it all in their hands. Take this quinine, a big dose of it, and kill theirself. They done it. A lot of times they'd mess up. Oh, it's a sad story.

I did know at one time what the main theory was at *throwing* them babies. When they'd take quinine, they'd take a whole bottle of castor oil. That's for the baby to come out smooth, they say. Easy, you know. It wouldn't be hard coming out.

But you know, these [birth control] pills they take, I guess castor oil do as good as they did. You can take pills to keep

a laundry bleach

an abortifacient

63

sickly

from having babies. It destroy the baby that's going to be before it gets there. I wouldn't do that either. Well, it may not hurt some people, but it will hurt others. Cause people never will tell you the truth about things, but you have to evaluate things yourself. They say it makes some people fat, it makes some people *poor*, it makes some people nervous, it makes some people menstruate for seven, eight, fourteen days. Well, I've seen that.

Black people didn't know a thing about a diaphragm 20 ≣≣≣

Birth control—that wasn't in the makings then. I mean, the black people didn't know it. Poor people like me. There may have been some well-to-do people that knew about it.

You take my grandma and them. Birth control was out of their category, although they could have afforded it. The people in the country, in the cities, black people like me, didn't know a thing about no diaphragm. They were right here in Dallas.[27] It wasn't even offered in the clinic, cause if it had of been, it would have been offered to me. Cause I'm one woman that really needed it.

Fixing to have those babies I was having, didn't know what else to do. The white woman I was working for, Mrs. Norrell, she's dead now, say to me, "Annie Mae, I don't want you to have no more babies. You just can't have them. It's going to kill you." She got me my first diaphragm. Took me to the doctor herself.

c. early 1930s ?

We were taught that the more children you had, the better it is for you. You change life better and everything. Now this is a silly thing, but there is a lot of things you hear if you deal with colored people. You see, I learned the hard way that the more children you had, the more it tear your resistance down. But I was taught different, that it don't hurt no one to have children, 10, 15 or 16 children.[28]

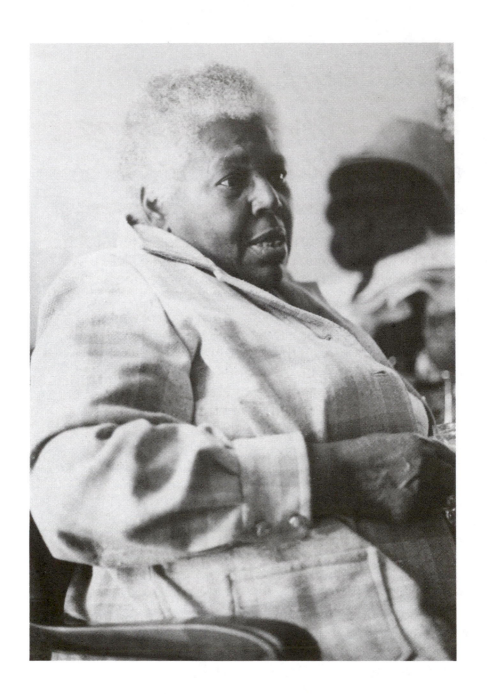

A fly couldn't stand on the collar 21

When I was raising these first three kids in Dallas during the Depression, after I had left my first husband, John Robert Prosper, I had jobs. Like mama, like daughter. I'd wash and iron. Like on Monday morning, I'd get up, I'd go out to Mrs. X's house, wash for her, hang her clothes up. Then I'd go on down to wash for another woman. I've done four washes in one day. I'd come on back, and these things I had just hung out for Mrs. X, they'd be ready. I'd take them down, and I'd sprinkle them and put them in a basket. And then she had other things for me to do. I could iron a shirt or a child's dress so a fly couldn't stand on the collar. A fly, he would slip off!

And then I'd go on down to this other woman where I just got through settin the washing, and I'd wash it out. Then if I had time to, I would go wash in another place, and stay there and take the clothes in. A lot of times, I'd have to look for places to wash. But I had these two regular places every Monday. Now I'd come back, and be ironing on the first wash I did. And I cooked. I was a very good cook. Everybody liked my cooking. I didn't have to worry about no jobs, because I always had a job as long as I was cleanin house and cookin. And I did that for a long time.

I worked for Mrs. Norrell for years and years and years, and whenever anybody would move, well, she'd always get me another job. She was very good to me. I couldn't have made it if it hadn't been for Mrs. Norrell . . . oh, I guess I would have made it. She'd get me night work, too, you know. Somebody would be giving parties. Oh, I worked extra many a day.

I'd go on out and clean a stove, a bad stove. My hands'd be all messed up. Cleaning an ice box. That's a day's work to clean a stove. But when you go clean this woman's stove, she don't do nothin in the house at all. Just clean a stove, that's work. That's a hard job. But in that day, you had to be at work at 7, 8 o'clock in the morning, and serve dinner at 5 o'clock in the evening. And sometimes if Mister So-and-So, whoever you worked for, would call and say, "I'm gonna be an hour late," you have to stay right there till he come home, and serve that meal. But you don't do that type of stuff no more. Sundays was the same thing. And you had to do it. If you wanted a job, you had to do it. If you get without a job, you'd see an ad in the paper, somebody'd want a maid, you go out there, there'd be 40 or 50 people already there. The employers really had their choice. The *pickaninny*[29] didn't know who was gonna be picked.

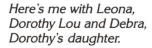
Here's me with Leona, Dorothy Lou and Debra, Dorothy's daughter.

JUNE 1963

I dressed a many a one of those girls asleep 22

Well, I'd go home at night, I been so tired, sometimes I wouldn't get home till 10, 11 o'clock at night, and I would start combin on one's head, comb my girls' hair. They had hair hang down to here. I'd comb those head of hair, and I would tie it up till the next morning. I leave her across my lap here combing her hair, and I would fall asleep, just dead asleep. I went to sleep a many a day with this child between my legs. I'd just sleep right in that chair where I was, and she lay down on the floor. And she's asleep and I'm asleep, and we stay that way all night. And I woke a many a day, and she was laying on the floor dead asleep.

But sometimes I had to get up at 3 or 4 o'clock in the morning, and comb their hair. Even if I had gone to bed at 12 o'clock, I got up. When I had to wash and iron, I'd get up before day and comb my children's hair. I dressed a many a one of those girls asleep. Lay them back down. Go tell my neighbor, Miss So and So, "They're already ready. Will you wake them up? And see that they get to school in time?" Many a day, I had to leave for work before they were up.

And this is the reason I tells my kids, "You don't need no *certain* somebody. You need *somebody*. Somebody. That's all you need. You don't need Susie cause she's actually your daughter. You ain't got to have Lauretta, your aunt; but you got to have somebody that cares." I always lived around somebody that cared. I would leave my children asleep, and they would go ahead and wake those children up. I'd talk about my

69

little Three Bears a lot of times. I'd have their little old meal here, I know what each one likes, and when they wake them up, they would eat their little food and go on to school.

They took their lunches to school, just like I did. The first children, I made their lunches every morning before I left. These last children, they would have free lunches at school. Oh, I was used to getting up 4:30 in the morning, 5 o'clock. That's the reason I sleep so late now. Well, I didn't think anything about it. That was the way of life with me. That's the way I had to live.

1930s

1940s, 1950s

Now here's Big Mama, she's holding one of her kids. She's Dallas's Big Mama. A whole lot of people's Big Mama. Lusettie Williams.

Big Mama cared about my children 23

Another thing now, when these three older children got up big, me and their daddy, John Robert Prosper, separated. They lived with him and me. That's the way we got the divorce. We had part-time children; part of the time they were with him, but most of the time they stayed with me because they were going to school. Esther, the oldest, she was a regular old mama to the other children—Dorothy Lou and Doris Minola. And Esther was their mama, truly their mama. Whatever Esther said went. Doris Minola—we called her Uncle Minnie, that's her grass roots name. Uncle Mineola, a woman, was the nickname of my neighbor, so when my baby Doris was born, Uncle Mineola asked me to name Doris after her, and call her Uncle Minnie. Which we do. If I say "Doris," nobody know who you're talking about.

Sometimes I wonder how did we make it. A lot of time, I'd come home and catch my door open, with the children's key around their neck. I'd talk to them about it. I'd whisper, "You all left mama's house open this morning. Think about that. Some day we might come home and find everything gone."

Well, I'll tell you. People wasn't like they is today. You didn't have to worry about your little girl being raped, and somebody breaking the house on them, because that wasn't the way of life then. It's the way of life with a lot of people now. They live by breaking on little girls, raping and stealing and killing. I don't know what happened to people.

interesting — compartmentalization

When I was working, the children had to wait till I come home for supper. Now Othella and George, they're six years apart, and Leona, they're all six years apart. Before Leona was born, I come home many a night, and George and Othella, they'd be at the door laying down asleep in the summer time. I always told them to go in the house, or go next door to Big Mama, my neighbor. But sometimes they chose not to; I'd come home late at night, and see Big Mama's window cracked like that. She'd be sitting at her window looking at them. Now she cared about my children. That's the reason I love her. And she wouldn't move them. She'd let them lay right there in the summer time, but she could see them. She set in there looking at those kids, and stay there until I come, and nobody didn't bother them. "Well, I was watching them. I sees who it was. I was watching you come. I'm going to bed now."

She's living today. Still over in North Dallas, in the rent houses. She cared, and I shares what I got with her right this blessed day. A lot of times she don't need nothing cause she lives better than I do, but to appreciate her, I want her to have something. I want her to know I'm thinking about her. If I go up to her and say, "Big Mama, I been thinking about you," she don't know if I been thinking about her or not; I may just be saying that. But when I take something over there, what she like, a pretty corsage or something for her to put on, she know I'm thinking about her. Right? So that's the way I do her. She said here a while back, she wanted a dark colander, the one with the legs on it. I went out there to K-Mart, they had one for a dollar. I went over there one day, and she wasn't there, and I put it on her door. Well, now, she loved that. See, now she can't tell nobody that she *thought* I was thinking about her. I don't have to buy her no thousand dollar ring. And she appreciated that colander, she loved it. I'm always doing things for her, cause she loved my children.

Here I am in Lubbock
taking care of a white baby,
the baby of a friend of mine
who was visiting.

This is one of Mama's
friends down through the
years in Amarillo, Mama
Della Johnson. I called her
Mama Della. They danced
together in the Holiness
Church for years. They
could sure dance. Those
women had to have
religion. After my mama
died, I would always visit
her, but she's dead now.

In Lubbock we went to work for some people named Forrester. That's me wavin.

Mama had to support the family. And she did. She worked like a dog. Wash, cook and iron. Pick cotton. Chop cotton.

Didn't like that West Texas sand 24

About 1932 or 1933, I went out to Lubbock with
this man I was with, George Darden. Fore I left Dallas, I was
working for Mrs. Norrell out on Mercedes. They were oil people. She had me in her will, and I knew it. If I had stuck by her
like I should have, I would have been *made whole.* Instead of
that, I followed a man off. Infatuation. That's all it was. All of
the Norrells is dead now. Her brother, Mr. Henry, also had me
in his will. And Mr. Henry just cried when I left. He said, "Annie
Mae, I hate to see you leave. I think you're making a mistake."
And I was. I made a mistake when I left. I know that.

    We set up housekeeping in Lubbock, but I didn't like it out
there. Cold! And I didn't like that sand. That sand was something else. You know, sometimes we'd be playing cards and,
really, the cards just began to fade away in your hand. You had
to have a mighty good house for the sand not to creep in.
We'd sit up there playing cards with the doors open, and never
think nothin about it, till the cards began to fade away. It's not
that bad now like it used to be. They do things to the land
now like irrigatin it; the way they plow, this way and that way, to
keep the soil from rolling off of it. The land ain't bad.

    In Lubbock we went to work for some people named
Forresters. I got my first social security card out there. We
would go on cotton picks. You know, way back yonder, it was
hard to find a job. If you went to apply for a job, you would
find 15, 20 people, maybe more than that, already there. So
people like us started to help themselves by picking cotton.

early 1930s ?

church
expression:
redeemed or
saved

c. 1932–1936

75

The farmer provided housing for us, but when cotton pickin was over, we moved to town.

My mother was out there in West Texas. My brother, too. She lived with me for a while. Yeah, that's one reason why I was out there. Later, my mother died in Amarillo. Mama was 56 years old when she died. She didn't live long. I've already lived longer than my mama and daddy. We lived in that area about four years.

But I didn't like it out there. Cold out there. I come home.

1949
Daddy, d. 1953

Here I am taking care of Wally Meir.

I raised her little kids 25

And so I come back to Dallas from Lubbock. I had
the oldest three children with me. I never did go back to work
for Mrs. Norrell; I went to work for Mrs. Truett. And I raised her
little kids right here, Beverly Truett and Sambo Truett. Their
daddy was the nephew of George Truett, who the hospital is
named for at Baylor.

1936

    Sambo didn't want me to be black. He knew I was black,
but he didn't want me to have nothin black. Whatever his
mama would give me, say she wanted to give me a scarf, it
had to be white. Any little way he was showing me, he wanted
me to be white. She couldn't give me nothin that wasn't white
till he was a big old boy. Sambo Truett.

    I worked for them, oh, I don't know, just a long time, till
they was about grown. Ten, fifteen years, something like that.

c. 1936–1946
or 1936–1951

And I raised Mrs. Truett's little kids, Sambo and Beverly Truett. Sambo didn't want me to be black.

That's my nephew on the right, Harliss McDade, and a friend.

On the right is my step-daughter, Verdell Darden, with her friends.

This is Quillar Darden, my brother-in-law. He was a pullman porter from Fayetteville, Texas. Now he lives in Utah.

1941 — that's when work began to go up 26

I lay right here in Dallas and worked for 3 and a half a week. Nineteen forty, 1941, that's when housework begin to go up. The Depression had sort of gotten over with. Things had began to go up, but it got to a standstill after a certain time. When Pearl Harbor got bombed, I was working right off Douglas, and I was making a dollar and a half a day.

And I fried pies after work too. At Nall's Pie Shop on Wall Street, at night from 8 to 12 o'clock. I was making 8 dollars and a half a week, and I had everything I needed. That's true. I had a diamond ring, fur coats. The fur coat I remember now was about $45 or $50. Course I didn't know anything about no mink, and I don't know if it was mink or not. I don't know what kind of coat it was. Only I knew it was a fur coat, and everybody was wearing em. It looked good at that time and I made 8 and a half.

I remember when my husband, George Darden, took 10 dollars a week. Worked for the Sinclair Station there on Boll and Ross Avenue. That was a great salary. We was making money.

And then after the war began to come, we began to make 5 dollars a day, 7 dollars a day. Now the girls gets 25, 30 dollars a day. Yeah, cause I went out to work here about three weeks ago on my cousin's job, I got 35 dollars and car fare. And they didn't work me as hard as they used to work.

So I've seen change now.

c. 1942–45

1977

79

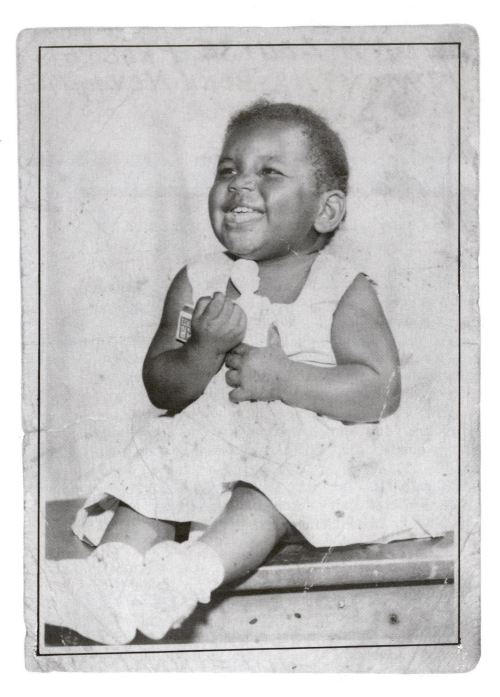

The doctors said I wasn't pregnant. A big growth. It was a growth all right! That was my baby Leona.

The doctors said I wasn't pregnant 27

Yeah, this last baby, nobody wanted me to have it. I didn't either. I didn't know I was pregnant with it. Now I was 44. Very unusual. For about, oh, four, five months, I never would see nothin. Well, I thought then I was changing life, that's what they say. So, in the meantime, I got pregnant one of these times, and I didn't know it, and the doctor didn't know it. He told me I wasn't pregnant. And, of course, I was glad to hear that. And Dr. Spence, he's one of the best urologists in Dallas, say he was going to *move* the kidney, had to *move* the kidney.

But Dr. Foler, he was a tall black-haired man at Parkland Hospital, he was an intern there, and he said I was pregnant. Said this is one of these pregnancies the mother don't know it herself until she get in labor. But Dr. Spence didn't believe it. I said, "Well, you'll get the tumor or the baby, one." He said, "I'm sorry, we're not cuttin high, we're cuttin low, and if there's a baby there, when we get through. . . ." I went to the hospital and had my operation in July or August; had my kidney *moved* out and I went to the O.B. Clinic in September, and they still said I wasn't pregnant. A big growth, and it was growing. It was growing fast. And the doctor was for getting it out as fast as he could. It wasn't no heart beat. That's what puzzled them.

Finally, in October, they decided my last pregnancy wasn't a growth. And the baby was born on the 19th of November, Leona was born. It was a growth all right! That was my baby. And I was 45.

1953

menstrual period

remove

*Every now and then
somebody would pay me
50 cents to make a dress,
cause that was a way of life,
and that was money.*

I never intend to clean nobody's house again 28

I had cleaned houses all my life. That's all I knew.
And every now and then somebody would pay me 50 cents
to make a dress, cause that was a way of life, and that was
money. I knew I could sew, but I didn't trust my mind at
sewing, cause I heard people say that people bring stuff to you,
and won't come back and get it out. Well, if I was making my
living off of sewing, I wanted my money when I got through.
With the children, I had to have money.

Well, I was doing housework, working for 5 dollars a day, 1955
and I was downtown trying to wait for the Preston Hollow bus.
I was outside H. L. Green—only they didn't call it H. L. Green,
they called it Seals and Grant—and I was on the streets slippin
and slidin on ice. A girl said to me, "If you go into Seals and
Grant and get you a pair of heavy socks and throw them over
your shoes, like I got, you won't slip and slide no more." She
had a pair of socks over her shoes.

I was in a hurry, trying to wait for the bus, so I went in
there and got me a pair of socks, and when I went in, I didn't
pull my coat off like you usually pull your coat off, so when you
get back outside you won't get cold. I went in there and got
me a pair of those socks, and come out. I didn't put them on
in the store, because I was scared I'd miss the bus, and I was
going to put them on in the bus.

When I got back outside, woman, I got so cold, it just
went through me. I started shivering; I just couldn't hold my
teeth. And my conscience, my mind begin to talk to me.

Which it do. It sounds a little silly, but it's true. I don't know if your conscience talks to you or not. And it says to me, "Good as you can sew, good as you can sell Avon (I had been selling Avon and I had quit), you ought to freeze to death." My mind is saying that.

I heard my own self's mind, and I said to this girl, "Now, I'm going back home." She said, "You're not going to work?" And I said, "No. No, baby, I don't have to do that. I've got on my best coat, but I don't have to do that. And freezing cold like I am? I never intend to clean nobody's house in this town, or wherever, or nothing, as long as I live."

I come on back home that day, and I called the Avon representative. And the next day I walked up on Bexar Street, and had this man to make me a sign, "Dressmaking," to put in my yard, and I went to making dresses and selling Avon. From that day I sold Avon up until . . . sold Avon 19 years. It ain't been long since I quit, about two or three years ago.

1974–1975

Selling Avon, I went from door to door.

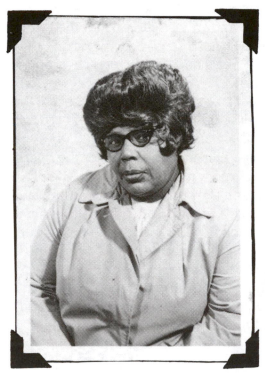

I would sell $900 worth of Avon in two weeks 29

Selling Avon, I went from door to door. No, we
didn't have parties, but I'd have coffee a lot of times for the
girls and me. I made nice money and would be selling it till
yet, but I can't drive, and I can't walk anymore like I used to,
and so I had to lay it down. I can't tote those heavy bags. I
used to get out here, and deliver those bags of orders.

I started selling Avon during the time that housework begin to go up. When I started selling Avon, we were getting 5
dollars a day for housework.

I would sell 8 or 900 dollars worth of Avon in two weeks
time. I would only get 40 percent of that. I had to take everything out of my 40 percent, like my orders, and I didn't understand exactly how to put this money in the bank and write a
check. I didn't understand how to do that then; and although I
had money in the bank, I was ignorant. I would buy those
high-priced money orders. Sure did. Some months, I'd make
better than 300 dollars. And that was money then, a whole lot
of money. That wasn't no drop in the bucket at that time.

The average order was 3 to 8 dollars. You would hate to
see some people order more than 8 dollars, and you would
hate to say, "Don't get it." You get to know, and when I go
home a lot of times, I would cut their order out. You know she
wasn't going to get it. When they come up, I'd say to them,
"You know, the factory didn't have it. They sent me a note on
it." Because I just knew better than to order 8 dollars worth of

stuff for Susie. Your common sense teaches you that. But sometimes they'll fool you. They come for it. And you didn't have it.

sickly As time went by, I got *poorly* so I did what I could.

I bought this piece of ground here and I built on it.

Leon Hunt and me in front of our house

Where are you going to get the money to buy a piece of ground? 30

I bought this piece of ground here, and I built on it.
Before I got this house, the last place we lived was in the
projects—Rhodes Terrace. That's where Leona was born. In
the meantime, I had gotten married again—Leon Hunt, Leona
and Othella's daddy. I said to him, "You know, we ought to get
a house, I'm tired of living around. I been movin' all my life."
And he said, "Well, hard as times is." I said, "Well, we can buy
a piece of ground, and as time goes on, we can build a
house." He said, "Where are you going to get the money to
buy a piece of ground?" I say, "I got a 100 dollars." And I
showed him the 100 dollars, and he liked to fainted.

We give a 1000 dollars for this here land. My husband's
sister gave us $300, but we were still lacking $600. Well, my
husband was working for Julius Schepps, and he lent us the
other $600. We bought it in the spring of 1954, cause Leona
was born in 1953. And then it set here for a while.

Well, we paid Schepps back the $600, and then we got
ready to build the house. The land was standing collateral
for the house. So my husband goes to Metropolitan Loan,
and talks to them about loans, and they say, "You don't owe
enough money." A lot of people think, cause you can't get
credit, you must owe somebody. You don't have to owe nobody. My husband didn't owe enough.

So, now, meantime, Julius Schepps, had his money in
everything. Anything that's worthwhile, Julius Schepps, he got
an interest in it, you can believe that. Me and Leon went down

a Dallas business
and community
leader for whom
the Jewish
Communtiy
Center was
named

and talked to Mr. Julius. I had worked for Julius when his two children was little, and I was a young woman. I said, "The bank told Leon he doesn't have enough credit." My husband doesn't talk very much. And I said, "We need a house. I needs a house, Mr. Julius. I want to know what you can do about it. Sign a note for him." Mr. Julius said, "Sign a note for you? Reckon Leon is worth me signing a note for? Gal, I don't see why you and those children can't have a home." Mr. Julius always called me "gal." When those children were little, he called me "gal."

He picked up this phone right there and called the bank. "Leon Hunt was down there trying to get a loan from you people." Told the bank who he was—Julius Schepps. And say, "I wants him to have that loan." That's all he said. And the banker called me and said, "Mrs. Hunt, Mr. Hunt was down here this morning. I think we can give him that loan. Let him come on back down." Now, the banker didn't know that I had been at Julius Schepps' and hearing what he said.

Now this house been here since 1960 and it ain't fell down.

He didn't want to put in no medicine cabinet 31

In the meantime, this very precious old white guy,
Worley, lived out on Peachtree Street, he says, "I will build you
a house for $4,000, and fix it like you want to." So we say,
"O.K." Believe it or not, I got this house built for $4,000; and
that was a break then, and it's a devil of a break now. Now this
house been here since 1960, and it ain't fell down. Ain't nothin
weak about it.

And that old man had all this lumber at his house. He
said he didn't know what he would do when he got too old to
build things. He went and bought materials down at these
freight companies where they sell sheet rock. And he had
sheet rock stacked that high in his house. He built houses
cheap.

I got five rooms here. If I had had a little more wisdom, I
would have built it different. It's built horrible, but I like it now.
See, we only got one drawer in the kitchen. Well, I been livin
with that one drawer so long, I don't know about having another one. And if I had of known, I would have had this for
a dining room, and that den would have been a kitchen—I
would have had a den on the other side. But I was so glad to
get it for $4,000, I got what I could, and I didn't worry about it.

The only thing, he wanted to put me a heater setting on
the floor, and didn't want to put in no medicine cabinet. I
wanted a heater in the wall. I said, "Now I draw the line right
here, Mr. Worley. I must have a medicine cabinet, I must have
my heater in the wall, and then I'll have a modern house." It

I got five rooms here. It's built horrible but I like it now.

would be, I call it, a *poor man's paradise*. So he added those things. And that sink didn't cost him nothin. It's chipped over there on the corner, just like it was when he put it here.

But I enjoy it. Cause we didn't have no money. We borrowed the money from Metropolitan Loan, and then paid them off. This house been paid for a good while. And me and my husband separated while he was paying for it. And when he finished paying for it, he come back and give me the deeds from Metropolitan Loan.

So I'm here, happy. I don't have no house payment. But I have a hell of a light and water bill to pay. I don't know what happened. I had them to put a new meter in, and my water bill this month is $22. No, don't even water the yard. Well, they can't find any leak. To trace it, they've got to dig all that pipe up out there in the streets to see if my water line is mixed up with anybody else's. The people from the city don't care. They say, "We're working on that. We are this and we are that." And my water bill this month is 22 dollars. You know, I'm thinking about filing suit against them.

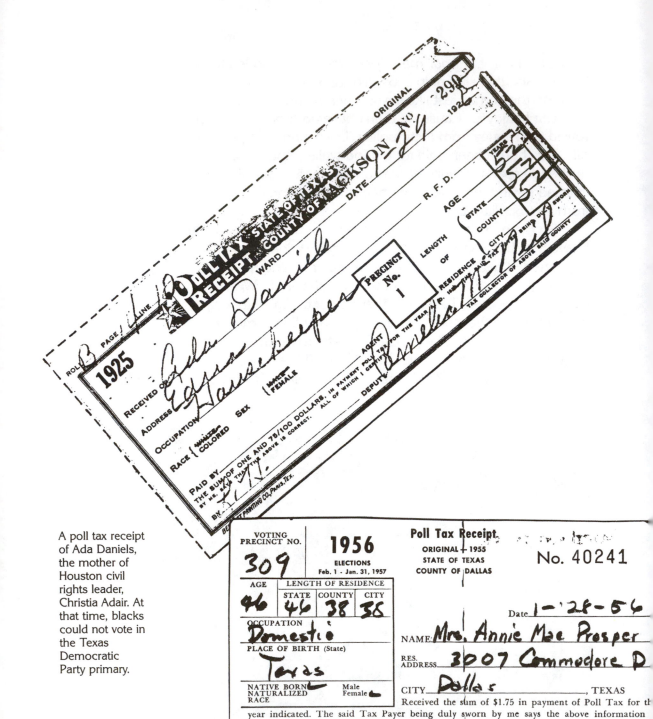

A poll tax receipt of Ada Daniels, the mother of Houston civil rights leader, Christia Adair. At that time, blacks could not vote in the Texas Democratic Party primary.

I wrote many a, many a poll tax 32

I got involved in politics when Othella Ann was about
two years old, I think, about 1949. I worked for a good many
years as a clerk at the voting polls in my precinct. I never was
a precinct chairman. I just worked with my precinct chair-
men. I do a whole lot of working in the Democratic Party, and
then I do absentee voting at the courthouse. I'm planning right
now to go to the Record Building next month to do a little
absentee voting.

1977
as a paid clerk

I wrote many a, many a poll tax.[30] I used to write them all
the time before I left North Dallas. I got into that through Mr.
Lott, Lott's Funeral Home.[31] He was very interested in politics;
he used to write them all the time on Commerce and Olive.
He was a deputy, and he'd come and bring me a poll tax book,
and I'd always write, and I've wroten thousands and thousands
of dollars worth of poll tax at a dollar seventy-five.

When I moved out here, in the project, Mr. Merchant, he
was the manager, he'd say, "Mrs. Prosper, I want you to come
up here and write the poll tax. These people up here in this
project are doing everything, going everywhere. They got the
best-looking cars, and I don't know where they coming from, it's
supposed to be the lowest paying in Dallas, but we got more out
here than anybody else.[32] Come out here and write these poll
tax." I'd sit there in the office and write poll tax, and, of course,
since then, I've wrote voters' certificates. I'm deputized.

At first, the people couldn't understand voters' certificates,
cause they were used to buying poll taxes. They just refused

93

to take those things free. But now they begin to understand it more better.

Blacks haven't been too long voting in the primaries.[33] Until 1944, we only voted in the general election. No, I don't remember when blacks couldn't vote in the primary. I was old enough to remember it, but it wasn't on my mind. I remember one time my mama left here and went down to Navasota, that's when she got into that trouble. Down there they load those black people up in a truck, and the man would tell them, "I want y'all to go to town and vote for Mr. Truett." Now this would only be in November, cause in the primary they wasn't allowed to vote. I mean now that's sort of sad to think about it. That's facts. I don't know how they did it. Evidently they must have bought the poll taxes for them, because I don't think the other fella would let you put a bunch of people in a truck, and go out and vote for Susie and you runnin, unless they were doing it right.

Me and Eddie Bernice Johnson the day she spoke at my Elks lodge banquet. I presented her with flowers. Down at the bottom is Daughter Hunter, our State President.

I did most everything to help out in politics 33

After the Second World War was when I first started
knowing anything about politics. That was a long time ago,
before the black man ever had any part of it. I was married
to a man named George Washington Darden, my little son's
daddy. We lived down in Granger, Texas. They gave big bar-
becues down there for politicians. I worked for Miss Merle, and
she was the one in the neighborhood that did all this cooking.

Nowadays, they give a little barbecue, and get somebody
like Jetton's to come out there and serve it. But then they
would dig holes in the ground and barbecued one or two days.
They didn't barbecue on top like you do now; but used to,
they'd dig holes and put chicken wire on top of it to hold your
meat, and you had the real McCoy.

After I had come back to Dallas, and as the years went by,
I sort of settled myself down. I began to help a little with Dr.
Howell in North Dallas. He was a precinct chairman, and after
I moved to South Dallas, he told me to get in touch with Mr.
Ernest Dillard, so I did. Mr. Dillard was a precinct chairman,
too. And after that, I got into politics a little at a time, and when
I knowed anything, I was just into it. I got acquainted with
Frances Dirks, and the man that was precinct chairman then
put her into the job after him. It was just like a *follow*, and I just
followed her. And now I know pretty well all the people—all
the interesting conservatives and liberals.

I didn't do no kind of secretary work, cause I'm not qualified
for that, but I did most everything else to help out in politics. I'd

work hours, stuff envelopes, lick stamps, and put stamps on, and do anything that needs to be did. I helped such mens as our junior congressman now in Washington, D.C., Jim Mattox, who I'm very proud of. He's a very good person. I've helped Mike McKool in his races for U.S. Congressman, three times in his trying to get in. Each time he lost, you know. And, of course, I did help him when he got in to be state senator, and just a whole lot of people that I worked for. Such people as Bill Bracklein, Larry Murdoch, and Tom Ellis—he's dead now—and Sheriff Jones and Congressman Earle Cabell, all those people.[34]

1977

And Eddie Bernice Johnson, that's the baby of them all. I've always had respect for her. Eddie is a beautiful woman, from a moral standpoint and everything. She got just enough pride in her to treat everybody right, not to stoop, but to be on a level with everybody. She was sworn in today as the Regional Director of HEW. I just left there this morning.[35] When I first knew her, she was a nurse and had a little son, and he was

Joseph Califano, HEW Secretary

there for the swearing in. Califano came down from Washington, but the Divine Sarah[36] swore her in. I call her the Divine Sarah. It was beautiful. Judge Hughes cracked a cute joke there this morning about Eddie just fixin to walk over the threshold into all she's in. But first, before she took the oath,

Krueger lost

Eddie endorsed Bob Krueger. He's running for U.S. Senator in John Tower's place. He's from New Braunfels, but he was there this morning. That was a big laugh. I know she couldn't have endorsed him after she was sworn in.[37]

Ann Richards won big in her race for State Treasurer. That was sure nuf beautiful. I spoke for her myself in getting the Black Caucus to endorse her. Our first woman Treasurer.

96

Wednesday morning

Austin American-Statesman

Cloudy, cold
Chance of rain, 60 percent
High: upper 50s. Low, mid 40s.
Gusty winds. Data A2

November 3, 1982　　☆☆ Vol. 112 - No. 101　　© 1982, Austin American-Statesman, all rights reserved　　25 cents

White looks like a winner as Democrats sweep state

Inside

- Bentse...
  as anger at ...
- Smith ...
  in District 4...
- Early t...
  gett, B4
- Renfro...
  seem headed ...
- Senate 1...
  ballots for late...
  B3

Staff Photo by Mike Boroff

The joy of winning

Democrat Ann Richards, trying to become the first woman elected to statewide office in 50 years, easily outdistanced Republican opponent Allen Clark in their race for the post of state treasurer. A Republican supporter, Mark Spaeth, shared in her joy at Richards' headquarters Tuesday.

Travis vote count marked by big turnout ...

By JOHN C. HENRY
American-Statesman Staff

Democrat Mark White appeared headed for the governor's mansion early today as Republican Gov. Bill Clements' $12 million re-election campaign came up short of votes.

White was being swept toward the governor's office on a wave of Democratic support for a long slate of statewide candidates that included U.S. Senator Lloyd Bentsen and Lt. Gov. Bill Hobby.

With about two-thirds of the state's 6,535 precincts reporting, 54 percent of the voters favored White.

"If things continue as they have throughout the evening, Texas is going to have a new Democratic governor," White told about 400 screaming supporters who packed into the ballroom of Austin's Driskill Hotel just before midnight.

Outspent by Clements almost 2-to-1, White credited his apparent victory to active campaigning by Bentsen and Hobby and to a united Democratic Party.

The two incumbent Democrats helped draw a higher voter turnout than earlier predicted by Republican Secretary of State David Dean. The official forecast Monday put turnout at about 2.5 million, or 42 percent statewide.

Reports from around the state indicated that up to half the registered voters in several East Texas and Central Texas counties braved wet, cold weather to cast ballots

Early returns showed White leading Clements about 4-to-1 in Harris County, home of ...

Staff Photo by Zach Ryall
Mark White and wife Linda Gale greet campaign workers.

Loving's cup is running over at ballot box

MENTONE (AP) — Officials in the nation's least populated county said Tuesday they have no explanation why there are 96 registered voters in a county that has 81 residents.

"Don't ask me," said Loving County Clerk Edna ...

Leste...

Controver...

NORMANGEE ...
versial South Texa...
ter Roloff and fo...
Tuesday when ...
crashed en route ...
preaching engageme...

Roloff, 68; Elaine ...
Susan Lynn Smith...
Palmer, 24, and Eno...
of Corpus Christi, d...
single-engine plane f...
ing crashed in a fiel...
north of Normange...
miles north of Housto...

Wingert was a frien...
and the others worke...
Jubilee Home for Ladi...
lee Superintendent Do...

Roloff became well ...
ing an eight-year batt...
State of Texas over lice...
homes for wayward ...
Austin state district ju...
allowed Roloff to opera...
kah Home for Girls an...

SECOND SECTION
★★☆★★
Sports - Features

The Dallas Express

SECOND SECTION
★★☆★★
Sports - Features

DALLAS 1, TEXAS, SATURDAY, APRIL 6, 1963

Ralph McGill Reports

Africans Impressed By U S Role In James Meredith Case

(ANP WASHINGON BUREAU)

WASHINGTON — (ANP) - A famed southern newspaper editor just returned from a six-week tour of Africa said the one thing Africans appreciated and understood—about Meredith and Mississippi, was the Federal governments intervention in sending troops to protect James Meredith.

Ralph McGill, columnist and editor for the Atlanta (Ga) Constitution said Africans were stunned that the Federal government would do all that for just one man.

Reporting informally on his tour to some 30 employees and officials of the State Department, here in Washington, McGill said he had great difficulty getting Africans to understand the way America works.

He said he spoke to hundreds of college and high school students in the eight countries he visited, and nearly all of the students knew of Little Rock and Mississippi.

Although most of the students did not know exactly who Meredith was, his name and that of Mississippi and Little Rock, were symbols of a U. S. problem that did not fit in with their general image of the U.S.

Their problem was one of wonder, he explained, that such situations could arise.

Known as the "conscience of the South" and as a southerner who disagrees with southerners —"out in public', McGill said he tried to explain that Gov Orval Faubus, of Arkansas and Ross Barnett, of Mississippi, were violators of the law and that the Federal government treated them as such.

In Eastern Nigeria, he said students were aware of Negro college students, picketing a Baltimore theater, and of the "Atlanta Wall" erected in his own home town.

The Baltimore theater owner and the erectors of the "Wall" in Atlanta were symbols of resistance to a momentum of change, he said he told the students.

The Editor said he had to **accept to relate our historical process to many of the perplexed students when he explained that the 'Wall' in Atlanta (which barred Negroes from moving into a white area would come down by legal processes.**

He explained to them, he said, that the U.S. is paying a great and evil price for its system of segregation.

A high point of his trip, related McGill, was in Ghana, when he arrived there almost at the same time that drummer Cozy Cole an a jazz revue from the U.S. arrive.

Members of the Ghana Press (which he said was hostile to the U.S.) took them to their club and gave them a going-for nearly three hours.

Cole was asked if he played in states with segregation laws, and, although he answered that he did, McGill said the press did give the two of them a kind word in the papers.

Negro Heads Billie Estes Federal Jury

EL PASO, Texas — (ANP) - Robbin E. L. Washington a Negro served as foreman of a federal court jury of 10 men and two women that convicted bankrupt farm tycoon Billie Sol Estes of defrauding farmers and finance companies in a $24,000,000 mortgage racket.

Washington headed the jury becoming the first Negro to serve on a West Texas federal court jury. The jury deliberated 49 hours and 44 minutes before reaching the verdict.

Estes, who was found guilty on four counts of mail fraud and one count of conspiracy to commit fraud, faces a maximum jail sentence of 25 years.

Dr King Sr Sues For $100,000 Over Auto Injuries

PHILADELPHIA — (ANP) - Rev Martin Luther King Sr, 62, of Atlanta, filed a $100,000 damage suit in federal court here as a result of a traffic accident.

Rev King sought damages against the Yellow Limousine Service, Inc., an airport limousine company, for injuries sustained here July 12, 1961.

The clergyman charged he was riding to International Airport in a limousine when it crossed a concrete divider strip and collided with an automobile on Penrose Ferry Bridge.

Rejects King's Son At School; Trustee Quits

ATLANTA — (ANP) -- A member of the board of trustees of the Lovett School has tendered his resignation as a result of the refusal of the board to consider Martin Luther King III for admission.

The application for the 5-year-old son of Dr Martin Luther King Jr., was refused in a letter to Dr and Mrs King.

James M. Sibley, chairman of the executive committee of the Lovett School board of trustees, said that Cecil A. Alexander had submitted his resignation as trustee.

The board has not yet acted officially on the matter. Sibley said, but will probably do so at a meeting later this month.

J F K May Name Third Negro Federal District Court Judge

WASHINGTON — (ANP) -- **The nation's third Negro federal district court judge was expected to be nominated by President Kennedy this week for confirmation by the Senate.**

Atty Charles T. Duncan, principal assistant U. S. Attorney, if confirmed would become the first Negro to serve on the U.S. District court bench in the District of Columbia and the youngest. Duncan is 38.

The other two Negro federal district court judges are Wade W. McCree of Michigan and James B. Parsons of Illinois.

Confirmation of Duncan would also increase the number of lifetime Negro federal judges to six. The other three are William H. Hastie and Thurgood Marshall of the U. S. Court of Appeals, the second highest federal court, and Scovel Richard of the U. S. Customs court in New York.

Ban Jim Crow Off Base Housing Lists

OMAHA — (ANP) -- While Congressman Charles C. Diggs of Michigan was calling for action by the Defense Department against an alleged case of housing discrimination at Ernest Harmon Air Force Base in Newfoundland, the Urban League here announced that by Offutt AFB to discontinue the maintance of separate lists of off-base housing for Negro and white personnel.

Names 2 Officers To War College

Comdr Samuel Gravely 1st Negro To Command U S Warship Named

WASHINGTON (NNPA) — The United States Navy has broken with tradition and selected its first colored officers to attend the Naval War College at Newport, R.I.

The names of Comdr. Samuel Gravely, of Richmond, Va., and Lt. Comdr. George I. Thompson, of Los Angeles, appear on a list of officers scheduled to attend classes beginning in the fall.

Comdr. Gravely, a graduate of Virginia Union University, and the first of his race to complete the midshipman's school (1944), is the highest ranking colored officer in the Navy.

In January, 1962, he became the first colored officer in history to command a United States warship, when he was assigned to the escort vessel Falgout.

Comdr. Thompson, presently assigned to the Bureau of Naval Personnel, has served at sea on radar picket ships, escort vessels, and carriers. He is a graduate of the University of California at Los Angeles.

At the War College, Gravely will attend the senior command and staff course along with 135 other officers, while Thompson will join a group of 100 officers in a warfare course.

DALLAS — Mrs Minnie Nell Taylor, membership chairman of Maria Morgan Branch YWCA, presents Mrs Mae Richardson the cup for being high producer in the 1963 Membership Drive, as Rev C C Berry crowns her "Mrs YWCA for 1963." Rev. Berry was devotional leader during the drive.

Ministers Institute Stated

Young people will be fully represented at the Lacy Kirk Williams Ministers' Institute, scheduled to be held at Bishop College in Dallas from April 30 to May 3, according to an announcement from Reverend Dr Richard A. Roins of Bishop, institute director.

The Young People's Department has announced its theme as being "The Message of the Bible for Youth Amidst Today's Tensions."

Director of the department is Miss Mary D. Galloway, of Longview, Texas, who has served in this capacity since the Young Peoples Department was originated. Assisting her will be a senior at Bishop, Reverend John Mayshack. Mr Mayshack was recently approved as a participate in the "Operation Crossroads" program which will take him to Africa for six weeks this summer.

Pianist for the department will be Miss Sondra Jackson, a Bishop student from Omaha, who is a Religious Education major, while Miss Ruth Oliver, a Junior majoring in music will be the song leader. Devotional periods will be led by Miss Bonnie F. Pryor, a Dallasite who is a sophomore at Bishop, and Miss Susie West, a Freshman majoring in Religious Education.

Among the highlights for the young people will be the keynote speech by the Reverend W. Brown, Minister in the Antioch Missionary Baptist Church in Beaumont. This will be on Thursday, May 2, at 9 p m.

The program will include a seminar on Thursday, May 2, at 1:30 p m on the subject of "The Bible and Christian Ethics," with Reverend Manuel L. Scott, pastor of the Calvary Baptist Church in Los Angeles, California, as the speaker. Discussants will be Reverend Willie Smith, Reveren Thomas Brown and Reveren E. J. Barnes, all majoring in Religion an Philosophy at Bishop.

Moderators will be Reveren Mayshack and Miss Ellie Miles, a Junior Honor Student at Bishop from Angleton, Texas. She will also serve as a discussion group leader following the Keynote address. Other such group leaders include Miss Vera Williams from Hope, Ark Donald Carpenter, from Indianapolis, Ind and John Sharo from Denver, Colorado.

It Pays To Advertise

Corsicana Activities

CORSICANA — Rev G. J. Oates, pastor, delivered the message on Sunday at Grace Temple AME Church from the subject "The Requisites to be a Good Missionary."

At 3 p.m. Grace Temple worshipped with Wesley Chapel CME Church in its 2nd quarterly conference. Rev L. J. Ward, pastor of Cedar Grove AME Church, was speaker. Churches represented were Bethel AME, Wood Chapel AME and Cedar Grove AME.

The young people of Grace Temple are preparing for an Easter program.

The ushers at Sixth Avenue Baptist Church observed their annual day with a special program last Sunday. Rev R. L. Jones was featured speaker. Others on the program included Mrs R. Beans, F. Madison, Mrs F. Jefferson, Mrs Lovie Smith, Rev E. C. Reynolds, Mrs F. Quarles and Robert Beans.

Irene Bits

Mrs Katherine King, Reporter

IRENE — Mrs Jessie L. Johnson has returned home from a two week visit with her daughter and son-in-aw, Mr and Mrs Smith in Lubbock, Texas. The Smiths accompanied her home for a short visit.

Mrs Zenobia Dowd, who is employed in Hubbard, has returned to her home in Irene, where she is recuperating from influenza.

DELLA REESE AT COCOANUT GROVEE

Vocalist Della Reese moves into the Ambassador's Cocoanut Grove for a two-week engagement this month.

Miss Reese, featuring favorite songs in her top selling albums and singles, will be supported by humorist Corbett Monica. Miss Monica's new school of comedy includes comentaries on the day's events.

A former gospel singer, Miss Reese is also slated to appear at leading supper clubs throughout the nation.

BELAFONE ADDS DANCING TO SHOW

World famous folk singer Harry Belafonte will add dancing to his Greek Theatre show this summer. Belafonte, booked for four weeks beginning Aug 12, holds the Green Theatre record ($296,300 in three weeks).

Sulphur Springs Highlights

Mrs Corrie L. Anders, Reporter

SULPHUR SPRINGS — **Elder C H McNeece was absent from his post at Mitchell Chapel Church of God in Christ on Sunday, due to illness.**

The Federate Choirs met at Evening Chapel Methodist Church on Sunday at 3 p.m. with Mrs Catherine Perry, president in charge. Rev M. C Perry, pastor of Johnson Chapel CME Church, Paris, Texas was guest. O. A. Askew was presented as "Man of the Year" The service pin was presented to Mr Askew by H. W. Grays, county agent.

Darcus Circle met last week in the home of Mrs Jeffie Lowe. Esther Circle met in the home of Mrs Elizabeth Thomas. Lydia Circle met in the home of Mrs Nancy Kelly. Ruth Circle met in the home of Mrs Irene Smith.

Morning Chapel Baptist Church began the 2nd anniversary of its pastor, Rev C. C. Wright, on last Wednesday night. Rev C. Alexander, pastor of Prairie Grove, Baptist Church, Emory, Texas, Shiloh Baptist Church, Quitman, Texas and Galilee Baptist Church, Como, Texas, was guest speaker. Members from each church were present. Mt Moriah Temple, Commerce, was absent, but sent a contribution by Tommie Watson of Commerce Mitchell Chapel Choir was present, accompanied by Mrs Catherine Perry.

On Thursay night, Rev T. F. Strange and Mt Olive of Mt Pleasant; Olive Branch and Pleasant Hill of the city; and Rev A. D. Sanders were present. Both choirs, accompanied by Mrs Robert Lee and Miss Margaret Davis, rendered music. Rev T. Franklin Strange delivered the message.

On Friday night, Rev John W. Williams and Ebenezer of Wolfe City; Rev V. Minter and St Paul of Neylandville; and Rev J. M. Sims of Palestine were guests. Mrs Olivia Scales, principal of Lone Oak School and Rev Watson of Dallas were also guests. The anniversary was climaxed on Sunday.

The Sulphur Springs Home Demonstration Club met last week in the home of Mr and Mrs Alex Lowe on Lamar Street. Visiting guests were Robert Slaymaker and James Moore of Mt Pleasant. They brought information about the Commission of Texas Employment Service. Mrs Johnson also gave information to the club.

SULPHUR SPRINGS — Sunday afternoon closed the second anniversary of Rev C. C. Wright at Morning Chapel Baptist Church. Visiting churches and pastors were Rev Booker T. Lewis and New Hope of Greenville; Rev Dave Buford and Sunset of Mt Pleasant; and Rev S. M. Wright and Peoples Baptist Church of Dallas. Rev Wright was the speaker. Visitors from St Mark, Winnsboro, Como, Commerce and Greenville were also present. Rev and Mrs Wright received many valuable gifts.

Mrs Velma R. Minter gave the welcome. A vocal selection was given by Mrs Catherine Jones.

Mrs C. L. Anders attended the BM and E State SS and BTU Congress Board at Greater Bethlehem Baptist Church in Dallas, last week. Revs A. D. Hereford, pastor of Mt Golead Church of Lone Oak and Tranquil Baptist Church of Winnsboro and M. L. Bradford, pastor of Bethlehem Baptist Church, Terrell, brought impressive messages to the Board members.

Esther Circle met in the home of Mrs Ruby Finney last week. Ruth Circle met in the home of Mrs Era Petty. Lydia Circle met in the home of Mrs Imogene Thomas. Darcus Circle met in the home of Mrs Catherine Jones.

DALLAS— Other high producers of the 1963 Membership Drive of the Maria Morgan Branch YWCA are shown with Mrs Mae Richardson who was crowned "Mrs YWCA for 1963" for being top producer in the drive. Left to right are Mrs Travis Lewis, Mrs Faye Goldwaite, Mrs R A Lay, Mrs Richardson, Mrs Bessie Ransom (runner-up to Mrs Richardson), Mrs Roberta Jones, and Mrs Wilma Clark. Not shown on the photo is Mrs M A Barnett.

No Whites allowed 34

I belong to one of the biggest clubs in Dallas, the
Democratic Women of Dallas County.[38] If I don't pay my dues,
I ain't gonna be in that. My dues are due this month, but I'm
gonna pay them. I go every month. I'm a board member.
This time of year we have luncheons every month, and then
we have board meetings once a month. Well, I'm the Telephone Solicitor. I have to call up people, remind them of the
meeting, anything that we got going. You find out people will
hear you more the second time you call than they will the first.

The Texas Black Caucus.[39] It's black only. No whites allowed. We don't try to get people elected cause they're black.
We try to get them elected cause they're needed, and cause
they can do the job. Cause we don't want them if they can't.
We try to pick the best man and try to make it educational, so
people won't get mad cause we elect James and didn't elect
Henry, all that kind of stuff.

Now it's Democratic and Republican, but they don't want
it like that. They want it the Democratic Black Caucus. You
can't go in there and do your business, cause the Republicans
will go back and tell them what you're doing, so they're going
to have a meeting down here in Tyler in two or three weeks.

Used to, they didn't allow blacks to vote in the primary,
which that's when you should work. This is the time you should
vote, and you cull the people out, cause in November when it
comes, it's only this or that. I've always said we need more
than two parties. Now we are supposed to have three all the

*Here's a page from my
scrapbook in 1963.*

time. You know Wallace run on one of them. But it's never nothin to it. The Republicans and the Democratic is the only thing that's really standin out, but we really need four.

My precinct chairman lives down the street and of course she's a politician. Frances Dirks is a politician. But now these people like this lady across the street, now those people is gonna vote, that's all. They ain't goin nowhere. That's all they're gonna do, vote. If you ask, "When you votin?" "Well, I'll be there. Can y'all get me a ride?" And that's important, too. Votin is important, but most people don't do any kind of work.

Sometimes people in this precinct didn't have no place to vote when election morning come. We had two or three places, schools, church houses, vote anywhere we could. We didn't know whether we were going to be able to vote there or not. People insultin you.[40] These little churches, you go in the front of the church, and they don't want you smokin in there, all that kind of stuff. Anything can happen when you got a public affair. People come in votin, a lot of them come in with a bottle of whiskey and things. And we stayed in high water all the time, so they finally got us voting right down here at the H. S. Thompson School, which is very good and I am glad of that.

I'm the political one in church. I raise political subjects, who I'm going to vote for. Think before you vote!

SENIOR CITIZENS — Martin Frost opposed Reagan's plan to cut Social Security benefits and Martin has consistently fought to keep our Social Security program strong.

To Annie Mae Hunt
Thanks for
your good work
for Martin Frost

Jim Mattox

MATTOX DISTRIBUTES YARD SIGNS TO SUPPORTERS
Annie Hunt [left] and Frances Dirks [right] were among the first Mattox supporters to put a sign in their front yards. Both Annie and Frances have been active in local community politics and civic events for many years.

My congressman is a very nice fella 35

Well, I said all the time that I was going to the next
Democratic President Inauguration. In 1972, they got Nixon,
so I didn't go. But, of course, Carter was the next one up, and
I went, and the parade tickets was 25 dollars apiece.

So I wanted to go, and I said, "Well, now, my congressman is a very nice fella," and I worked for him down through
the times. He knew me by name, so I called Congressman
Jim Mattox. I said, "Jim, this is Annie." He said, "Yeah, what
can I do for you, Annie?" I said, "Well, I'm wanting to go see
Carter and I ain't got nothin to represent me with. Now, I'm
settin on your front door steps with my shoes unbuttoned, and
I want to know can you get me off your front door steps?" He
asked what did I need, and I said, "I got my money. I'm ready."
I wanted him to know he didn't have to pay for it. That may
hurry things up. So he said, "Annie, get off my door step, and
button your shoes up. You are on your way to Washington."

So about four or five days before I got ready to go, somebody knocked on my door. I said, "Who is it?" He said,
"Steve, from Jim Mattox's office." I just run grab up a 50 dollar
bill and gave it to him because that was my dance ticket, which
Carter called *party* ticket, and my parade ticket and my inaugural ticket to get into the grounds of the White House. You
can't go in the grounds of the White House just because you
want to.

inauguration of
President Jimmy
Carter, January,
1977

Carter is a Baptist

103

Senior Citizens, Mrs. Pearl C. Anderson, Chip Carter and Mrs. Annie Hunt, enjoying the company of the President's son in South Dallas.

I rode the Greyhound to President Carter's inauguration 36

I rode the Greyhound bus to Washington. I left here on a Monday night and got in Washington on Wednesday morning. I didn't have nobody to go with me, so I caught the bus and went on by myself. I met a very friendly woman up there. She's political minded too.

The first night I like to froze to death. Up there cabs is plentiful, but they don't take one person. I went to the White House entrance that is up from the Longworth Building where we was having the party that night before the Inauguration, and I said to the police officer, "You know, I can't get a cab. I'm freezin and I am from out of town, and I don't know where I am at. All I know is I'm on a hill here, and my congressman have already gone. I don't know where to call him at." And he said, "Where you from?" And I said, "Dallas, Texas," and he said, "Well, don't worry, I will get you a cab." So he called a cab for me, and I went back to the Holiday Inn.

On Inauguration Day, I was right in the grounds. I was right down there looking up at Carter. He was up high, you couldn't see too much; the pictures I got, nobody know what they is but me. Cold? It was so cold that I didn't even know when people stepped on my foot. I was glad cause I know my foot is still alive. Boy, it was cold. I had to brush ice from under my feet to see the Inauguration, and after all this was over with, here come Billy Carter out, and there was two guys there sitting next to us from Georgia, and I asked one, "See old

Billy?" He says, "Yeah, I see old Billy. I was raised with him. Miss Lillian never could learn him no sense."

And, oh, we just had a good time there, and after the Inauguration, we turned out and went and got a little food, and they had buses standing there waiting to take us to the parade grounds. The route of the parade had big stands, as tall as that house high, and, of course, I had one of those seats for 25 dollars.

The parade came by. First of all, the White House staff and cars, and then the Mondales and then the Carters. I got a picture of the Carters in the parade when they were marching. I hollered, "Texas Airport." Then Jack Carter turned around, and the whole family tried to see who I was. Now, I had got some lovely pictures of Jack when he was in Dallas. I told him, "Dallas, Texas, taking pictures," and then he realized who I was. Boy, he was sure looking. Then the Carters got up in the grandstands, and set there and seen the parade. It was very nice.

Oh, the party that night was gorgeous. Just like this door was Union Station, on that side was a rock concert when you come in the door, and then when you come through this door, here was Duke Ellington's band, and thousands and thousands of people was there. Grapes and cheese of all kinds. Thousands and thousands of that stuff throwed away, just so sad people throw food away like that. Everything was very nice. President Carter and his wife and little girl came in, and they said he danced a little, but I didn't see that.

"The inaugural parade route stretched before us with tens of thousands of people lining the streets."
—*Jimmy Carter*

I was waitin tables at the Elks on week-ends. That was my job. I was getting paid for it. I'm on the left.

I shall never be nothing but an Elk 37

I ride the bus all the time. I went right back to
Washington last month for the Elks Convention. I goes every
year. I have gone every year since 1963.

1977

Daughters of I.B.P.O.E.W. That stands for Daughters of
Improved Benevolent Protective Order of Elks of the World.
The Daughters of Elks is 75 years old, and my temple is 40
years old or older. You see, our part is known as a temple, and
my particular temple is Sunrise Temple. We got our Daughter
Ruler and Vice Daughter Ruler and Assistant Daughter Ruler.
The mens have the Grand Lodge; then they have an Exalted
Ruler, an Esteemed Leading Knight, and a Second Leading
Knight. Beulah B. Kelly is secretary and will be until she dies.

The white lodge is not "I," they're just "B." The white
lodge only have B.P.O.E.W., Benevolent and Protective Order of
Elks of the World. And there's a story behind that. Years ago,
they wouldn't let us join the Elks when we wanted to, so our
Exalted Ruler say we're "Improved." No, we're not a part of
their organization. We couldn't. We tried to be years ago, but
we are not a part of it. We're separate.

Now some of the white womens are members of the Elks,
and the one that Mike McKool belongs to out here on Ferguson Road, I understand that some of the women are in now;
but the one out here on Greenville Avenue, they're not. They
don't have any part. They're just the men's wives.

I love the lodge. You can believe me when I say that. We
have about 100 active members and we meet twice a month.

I ride the bus all the time.
I went right back to Washington last month for the
Elks Convention. Here I
am on the left.

This is a picture I took on
the Staten Island ferry in
1968.

We have a hall up here on Forest Avenue. We discuss things that we want to do, things that we want to continue. Or we are trying to find a better way to do what is already been done before, cause it just rolls over and over. What comes around goes around. Same thing each year, and we try to do things better. That is the way it is. And we meet our friends there. We have a junior chapter too. The boys are called Herds and the girls are called Juniors.

I got a service award for holding different offices, and raisin money. We have fund raisin. We give out charity. This is one of our mottos. All Elks throughout the world give away a whole lot of food to people that's needy on Christmas. We communicates during Christmas.

Now you take Eddie Bernice Johnson. I got her to speak in 1973 at our Elks Lodge annual banquet. People said "I didn't know she could speak like that." And I say, "You're right here in Dallas with her and don't know it." I knew she could. When I ran into our ruler in New York City, I asked her to have Eddie speak. So we did.

We had 800 people at the banquet, and she had everybody's eyelids raised up. At the Statler-Hilton Hotel in Dallas. We didn't have room for the people. Everybody heard she was gonna come speak, they tried to come because they didn't know she could do it. Now when I tell my Elks Grand Daughter Emma Kelley that Eddie Bernice Johnson is the Regional Director here of HEW . . . well, now, she's probably gonna be on the Elks agenda real soon again, maybe next year at our meeting in Atlanta, Georgia.

Roots, we have got them, too. I'm very much proud of this lodge. I love it. I would take nothin for it. I shall never be nothing but an Elk.

I shall never be nothing but
an Elk. This was in San
Antonio in 1974.

112

A man ain't going to have no baby 38

About the women's movement: I wouldn't participate in it. Cause I think you got to make up your mind and not be straddling the fence, and I am. There'd be so many no-nos until the movement wouldn't want me with it no way. Oh, yes, you know I was discriminated against. There's some things I'm for—I'm for pay—if I do the work that Henry do, pay me like you do Henry. But I don't want no equal rights. I don't want to be no man.

We're asking for equality, right? But you know we really don't want that. Why don't they come out and say just what it is? We want certain things. I'm a lady; I may get pregnant. I don't want to work like no man. Every time I was pregnant, I had to work until just about the time. I had to. I was strong as an ox, and I didn't have nobody to take care of me. I was always ironing. Othella was going to be born on the 18th of August, and on the 17th of August, I was wearing my uniform to go to work, and my water broke at the ironing board. I knew she was going to be born, but I had to work.

Now a man ain't going to have no baby. And I know some girls ain't going to have no babies. They're doing just like a man. Driving those big trucks. If I do the same thing Henry do, pay me. I'm cross the fence. Anything you say, there're going to be somebody for and somebody against. Let the ones that really believe in equal rights, that want that, let them get together. But I won't participate in it at all.

113

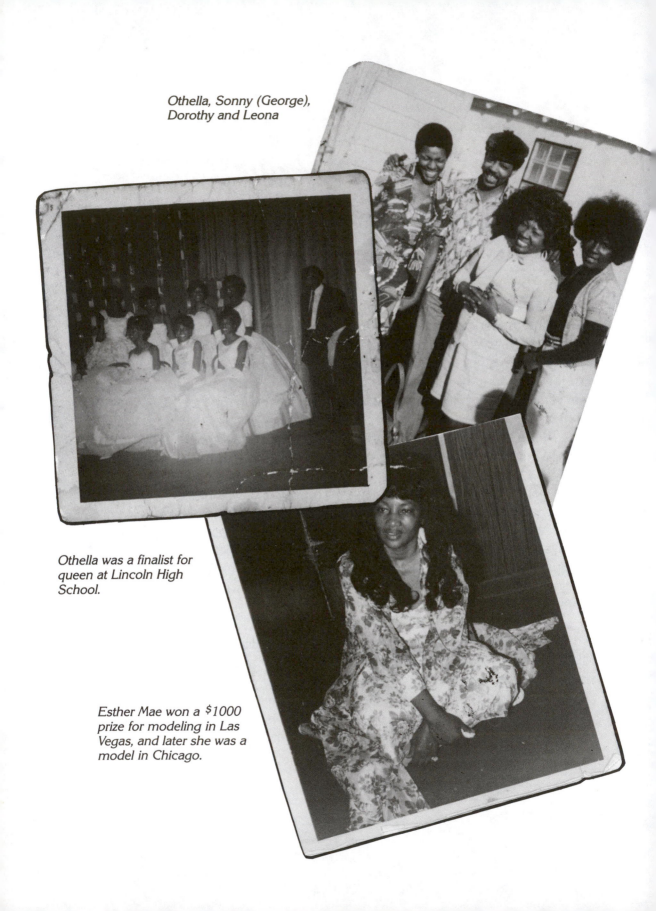

Othella, Sonny (George), Dorothy and Leona

Othella was a finalist for queen at Lincoln High School.

Esther Mae won a $1000 prize for modeling in Las Vegas, and later she was a model in Chicago.

I don't feel guilty no kind of way 39

I think the nature of my children—course they're all
grown now and got their own children—still, they're children
that love to work. I'll take that back. They know they have to
work to make things possible theirself, and they all live well.
Now, I ain't had none of my children go to jail. Yeah, I haven't
had to go to jail for nothing, to get nobody out. And I don't
think I done all that myself. I think it was the nature of the
child. There's plenty of children raised up right, they'll go
wrong anyway.

1977

I tried to send all of my children, that would go, to college. I know education ain't all of it, but you can do so many
things with education that you can't do without it. And I've
always wanted them to go as far as they could in life, cause I
never got no farther than the fifth grade. I've gone to school
since I was grown. I told my girls—it's very important they go
to school.

The baby here, Leona, she had more chance than anybody cause she could have borrowed money and gone to
college, but she didn't want to go. The rest of them, all went
but two.

Esther Mae and Othella both went to Prairie View. They
studied education, straight education, but none of them ever
did anything with it. After two years of Prairie View, Othella
quit, and later went to Texas Southern University in Houston,
and finished there. Now she and her husband have a karate
school in Houston. Othella do the business part of it.

Here's my baby Leona graduating from Lincoln High.

United States Marine Corps

Certificate of Acceptance

This is to certify that   GEORGE WASHINGTON DANDE JR   has successfully passed the required mental, moral and physical examinations and has been accepted for enlistment in the United States Marine Corps.

The defense of our country and our freedoms is the duty and privilege of every citizen. The Marine Corps has a proud tradition of outstanding service to our country in peace and war. Voluntary enlistment in this elite military organization is a clear demonstration of those American qualities of patriotism and loyalty to God and country.

Presented this FIFTH   day of   AUGUST   1958

By the Officer In Charge
Marine Corps Recruiting Station
DALLAS, TEXAS

JOHN D. FLYNN
CAPTAIN USMC

George went to the Marines when he was 16 years old, stayed in the Marines four years, and had two years of active duty.

Esther Mae lived in Chicago where she ran night clubs and was a model for about 27 years, and came home this past Mother's Day. She'd been trying to come home before then. She'd come and leave. But she say she's going to stay this time. She lives with me and works at the Adolphus Hotel as a waitress, but she's trained as a telephone operator.

George went to the Marines when he was 16 years old, stayed in the Marines four years, and had two years of active duty. Then he went to college somewhere in California. He lives out here in Oak Cliff. He have had one job in this town, working for the Post Office. He's a smart thing. Would never do his homework when he was young. He'd come into class and study and write down his homework, and everybody in the class said, "Give it to me, George. What did you get, George?"

Dorothy finished high school. She takes care of a community house sponsored by HUD or HEW, or "who," on Washington Avenue. She's active all day, teaching children how to play basketball and volleyball, and goes with them to Houston and different places.

Doris Minola lives in Houston. She's a seamstress. She sew in her home. Leona's on a new job, about six months old. Leona's the type that jump from job to job—they're all good jobs. Now she's at some kind of factory. She was working at one of these ones where they make these eye glass frames. She ain't there anymore. Sears and Roebuck, I tried to get her to stay there. She quit that. She went to Titche's and they didn't give her nothin and she left Titche's. I said, "See there, that's where you need your education that I wanted to give you." I told her all the time, "You're so much like your mama." My people wanted to educate me, but I seen a man I wanted, so now I ain't got the education or the man. She's just like her mama. She don't have the education now or the man.

I always wanted the best for my children. I wore shoes I didn't want to wear, eat what I didn't want to eat, cook what I didn't want to cook, work where I didn't want to work, and stay where I didn't want to stay, for them. I did it for every one of

them, and I don't feel guilty no kind of way. That's enough.
I tried to tell my baby the other weekend (she always wants
money), "I don't have no money. I'm going to play bingo tonight." Well, now, I can't give her my money. She's grown.
Let her get out and do for herself. I'm going to play bingo with
my money. And I don't feel guilty. But sometimes I'm weak. I
break down. She called me last night, said she wanted three
dollars, and I forgot to leave it and went on bingoing. Got way
out yonder in East Dallas before I remembered, and had to call
my next-door neighbor and ask her, "Say, Marie, will you give
Leona three dollars for me?" Done got weak, see. That's all
right. She's my baby.

*Me and Uncle Minnie. Now
she wants me to call her
The Queen.*

This is me with Leona's kids, Gus and Quashondra.

This here is Sonny (George), with his wife and their three sons.

I am broke out with grandchildren 40

I am broke out with grandchildren. I have 26 grandchildren and 22 *great* children.

Dorothy has got more grandchildren than anybody else; she has 11 children. Othella has one, and George has three boys. I got a whole lot of grandchildren older than my baby Leona.

A funny thing happened to these children. One of Dorothy's girls, Beverly, went to Thompson School. She decided that since she was eight years older than her Aunt Leona, that she was just too big to be Leona's niece. So she said, "Leona, I'll be your auntie and you be my niece." So Leona's first year in school, she thought that really was true. She come and told me her and Beverly had traded. Said she was going to be Beverly's niece, and Beverly was going to be her auntie. I said, "Honey, this happens all the time, and Beverly can't do anything about it."

Esther Mae has got three lovely boys. I raised one of them, Charles. I consider him my child. He lived with me all his life. When his mama had him, he was right in my house. Now he's in the U.S. Air Force. When he got married, I made all the nine girls' dresses for the wedding. The bride had a little flower girl, which was Othella's girl, and her cousin or her nephew was the ring bearer. I made her train, her veil. I made it all. You buy a streamer with flowers to go across there. She had had a baby, and she didn't want to be in white, so she was in blue. But she wanted a train, so I made a long train. It

121

Othella with her husband and Yolanda

This is Dorothy with her husband and three of their children.

Here's Doris and some of her grandchildren.

was beautiful. I made all of them's clothes. I didn't have any money to complete a wedding. I gave it to them for him; I didn't charge them a penny.

Doris Minola got six children and two grandchildren. She had a great tragedy not long ago. Her husband, they had been separated about seven or eight months, got burned up.

Leona has two children. Her son stays here most of the time. He said to me the other day, "Grannie, you love me?" I said, "Yeah." He said, "How come you hit me?"

Othella's daughter, Yolanda, her mama was in Prairie View when she was born, and I just kept her. And naturally I would yield towards her. If you have a little puppy around the house, you yield toward it—you got to feed it, you want to do for it, bathe it. I knew I couldn't raise it. I called her about 4 o'clock one morning. I said, "Othella, come get your baby. I'm not able to handle it. I can see her doing wrong, and I won't even try to stop her."

Well, I figure I don't feel bad. I did my share. I tried. When I had to wash and iron and get up before day and comb my children's hair. They all had long hair. I had to get up at 3 or 4 o'clock in the morning and comb their hair. I went to sleep a many a day with this child there sittin between my legs. I was asleep. I was so tired when I get home, I'd fall asleep. And I woke a many a day and they'd be asleep on the floor. And a lot of time I'd get their hair combed around 10 or 11 o'clock at night, and I'd tie it up for the next morning.

And my daughter Leona cut her little girl's hair, and everybody want me to say something about it, but I didn't. I felt it. And I say to a friend of mine, "None of y'all are going to go over there and comb that girl's hair for her. She get up in the morning and go to work. Nobody goin to comb her hair but Leona. Plaiting her hair every morning, braid it up."

So Leona cut her little girl's hair short like mine. Run a comb through it and forget about it. These white girls have their hair short. And I think she's the cutest thing. Everybody

think she's a boy. I took her to town with me Saturday. Me
and her mama went to town, and there she was looking like a
little boy, and she wears her brother's hand-me-down clothes,
boy's jacket. She has one of those little jean jackets. Just
can't afford to throw them jackets away. And she was the
cutest thing you ever seen with her jacket on. And a lady said,
"Oh, isn't that a cute little boy." And I said, "No, it's a little girl."

*Here he is with his girl
friend Linda.*

*I raised one of Esther Mae's
boys, Charles. When he
got married, I made all the
nine girls' dresses for the
wedding.*

This is my Aunt Sadie Davis.

This is Mary, an old friend of mine.

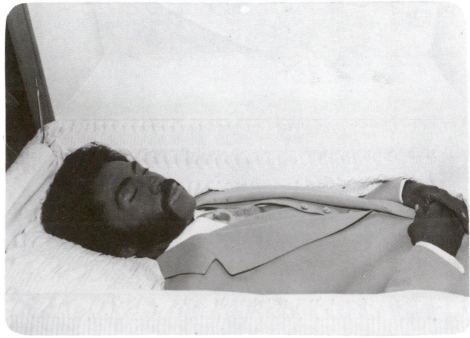

California was miles and miles and miles away, which it ain't nowhere now 41 ≣≣≣≣

When I was growing up, all my aunts and uncles moved away from Brenham, except my daddy's brother. Some of his sisters and brothers moved down to Waters, Texas; some went to Sealy, and some moved to Houston. They never did get very far. My daddy also moved away; he left my mama and moved to Houston. I had lots of aunts and uncles on each side, Mama's and Daddy's side. All dead. My last auntie died here about two weeks ago, my daddy's sister. Went to a funeral in Houston about two weeks ago.

Mama's brothers, some went to Amarillo; some went to Hobbs, New Mexico; some Wellington, Texas. One moved to California, and that was miles and miles and miles away, which it ain't nowhere now. That was so far. One moved to Mott, Texas—that was another distance. But it ain't nowhere now. Get in a car and get there in the next two hours. But that's the way it was.

And when I got home from homecoming last year, I got some phone calls. One old boy I seen there—he was my age, but he wasn't sick, doing all right—everybody called him Gramps. But yet they found him the Friday after homecoming dead in his house. And then I got another call, "Annie Mae, I'm calling you right back. They found your cousin this morning, Sambo Rogers Birch." He wasn't really a cousin, but his first cousin was my first cousin, and we knew each other all our lives. Found him dead.

127

OBITUARY

SFC Eddie Ray Eatmon, son of Edward Eatmon and Lillie May Whitfield, passed into The Great beyond, May 2, 1970, while serving his country in Viet-Nam. He was injured April 27. He was born August 23, 1935, and spent all his early life in this community. Graduating from Richard B. Harrison High School in 1954, and spent one year at A & T College before his enduction in the Army.

On May 13, 1965, he married Miss Alma L. Hamilton of Dallas, Texas. They made their home the Army.

He joined White Rock AME Church at an early age and faithfully attended church while at home and sent contributions to his church.

He was a faithful and loving husband and was always smiling and cheerful. He is survived by his wife, Mrs. Alma Eatmon, one daughter, Jacquline Eatmon, His father Edward Eatmon, his mother Mrs. Lillie Whitfield, six aunts, and a host of relatives and friends.

He served his country well, giving his life so free men and women might live in a democratic society.

ANOTHER SOLDIER GONE

Another soldier gone
To get a great reward
He fought the fight and
kept the faith
And now gone home to God

He fought until he fell
Upon the battle field
And then he heard the General say
"Lay down your sword and shield"

His soul has gone to God
The earth has claimed its own
And now he's shouting round the throne
While we are left to morn.

Someday we'll meet again
Our loved one gone before
Someday we'll reach that happy land
Where parting is no more

—Family

Eulogistic Services
For
SFC EDDIE RAY EATMON
August 23, 1935
May 2, 1970

Sunday, May 10, 1970
White Rock AME Church
Micro, North Carolina

Rev. Claude McAllister (Officiating)

Burial ... Smithfield, North Carolina

This is the funeral program for my niece, Georgia Mae Hall. She was killed in her house; had her head beaten.

In Remembrance

Comfort

There is a tower of strength
For you and me - -
'Tis that which we call faith
And as the sea
Oft dashes on the rocks
To no avail
So storms may come to us;
But in the gale
We lean upon that faith
And soon once more
We see a beacon light - -
It is the shore.

FRANKLIN LEE STEVENSON

GEORGIA MAE HALL

Born: September 27, 1931
Brenham, Texas

Died: December 19, 1970
Hobbs, New Mexico

Services:
Pleasant Green Baptist Church

Rev. H. R. Watkins
Officiating

Interment in
Everglade Cemetery

Pallbearers

Melvin Wornsley
Henry W. Williams
Jessie Nelson
Willie Smith
Jim Browley
Luke Ellison
Dave Risher

Once a year the peoples comes together

42

My church in Washington County is the Good Will

Baptist Church. I'm going there on the fourth Sunday in this month for my homecoming. I go there each year. I stays there till the first Sunday in October, stays another week for the Methodist homecoming, cause one side of my family was Methodist, and the other side was Baptist.

September 25, 1977

The churches are out in the country. In this country where I lived out there, they had a little place called Wesley, and they've got another little place down near my church called Welcome, that's a little town. And another village called Industry, no bus doesn't go through. Where these places surround, it's a community. There's plenty of black people, cause they own all that out there in the country around Good Will Church. They have a different mind from the black man up here; they didn't get rid of their property and move to town.

Austin County

I got a cousin right now who's building her a brick house out there on her daddy's and their place. They done divided it up, and she took up her part and is building herself a brick house; and her brother already built his house out there; and this is gonna be a regular community of brothers and sisters. That's out there where I'm going.

When I was little and we lived in the country, we went to church on Sunday, and we went to Sunday School. We never

My church in Washington County was the Good Will Baptist Church. I go there each year for my homecoming. That's the first place I went to school.

And not too far away was my daddy's church, Pleasant Grove Methodist. The churches are out in the country near Wesley.

My grandma and them are all buried there, right next to the church.

Dan McAbney, my childhood sweetheart

Cousin Mattie Randon and Mrs. Pruett in Dallas

got to Sunday School at 9 o'clock like they do here. It would always be 10:30 or 11 o'clock before we got to church, because we had to walk or ride in the wagon, ride horseback or something. When we get there we had Sunday School, then we'd go into church; we turned church out around 1 or 2 o'clock, and then we'd come home and eat. We didn't stay at church; we'd come home.

On homecoming, once a year the peoples comes together; and no doubt about it, when I get there people will be there, from California and everywhere. They say, "Well, I'm going home. Oh, I takes my vacation when I have a homecoming in my home town." And they do. They come home on that day.

It do something to you to go there. I couldn't stay away from there for nothing. I'd have to be sick to stay away. If my daddy was living, he'd be there. Oh, yeah, he'd be there. This auntie that's dead, is buried now, she won't get to come. She was always there.

It's beautiful. That Sunday, don't do a thing. Don't have no prayer meeting. Just have food, people there, there'd be stands, and they're not selling it either. All that food—they're giving it away. Homecoming.

We have everything to eat. Barbecue. Sheep. Goat. We had a goat somebody barbecued, beef, barbecued hot links, chicken, everything. We had some brisket meat, the best I ever eat in my life, down there. Yeah, everything was real nice. So much food left over. This girl that was there at the house where we go, she says that we could just give somebody this food. I said, "Well, that's the truth. Ain't there no hospital in town? Can't we give it to somebody?" If this was in the city, we could give it to somebody, but there in the country, she said, "Ain't no way to save it and people don't want it. People don't want no food."

Richard MacNeal, got this church up here on Oakland in Dallas, he's from the same place, and sometimes he goes there and preaches. Whenever they say, "Little Richard Mac-

This is Toad Mathis, and his wife is name Toot. Toad and Toot. If you say Leroy and Rosie Lee, nobody know who you're talkin about. These are my sure nuf folks, my real people. Anytime of the day or night I can go to them, sure can.

Neal is coming," boy, every *nigger* and his brother is there. They had a family reunion recently. I didn't get to go; but that was their family reunion, it wasn't the church's. Homecoming is the church; this is not a family reunion.

When I go, I stays with some first cousins in Brenham near Blinn College. Toad and Toot Mathis. I was raised with them. Brenham is a beautiful place; I never lived there till I was grown. You should drive through there and see the Negro homes. Beautiful. They had so many Negroes that lived in the country, they done moved to town now; and now they're moving back to the country. They didn't sell their property; now they're moving back. And this sister and her husband moving from Houston back. Got their business and everything, their barber shop there. They're getting old now. They worked like dogs all their life. Now they can make a home; that's what they're doing.

I don't want no man no more

43

You know, a long time ago I didn't buy clothes. I buy
things now because I want to. I buy this kind of stuff, denim
gauchos. I had no business buying this. I love this color. This
was 17 dollars and it don't fit. I have to take it back. And this
jacket crawls up and makes a fold across my shoulder, it's
ridiculous. I'm built just like a buffalo in the shoulders. I wear
boots and everything. Gaucho pants. I wear anything that
anybody else wear. I never could do it while I was young. The
only thing I don't have is a pair of jeans. I don't know if I can
wear jeans or not. I don't know if I would look good in jeans.

I specialize in making men's clothes. I made 17 suits for
a singing group of boys. I said to one of the men, "Do you
have a sense of humor? Are you married?" He said, "No." I
said, "Well now, can you come to me anytime I call you? If I
come home from bingo at 11, 12 o'clock at night, can I call
you over?" He said, "Yeah, if you'll let me sleep on the couch."
And all these boys call me *mama*. And sometimes he calls
me and says, "Mama, are you gonna need me sometime
around 1 o'clock at night?" And I said, "I might." It made me
so nervous after I finished all those suits. I was at the concert,
they were singing. I guess I was happy.

My first husband was a good man. I just didn't know how
to live with him. And when I decided I was going to live with
him, it was too late. I didn't have nothin to offer. Now me and
my last husband separated. I just put him out to stay a little
while when I found out he was shackin with a woman just

137

about seven or eight blocks from the house here. And then my shackles fell.

I don't have anything to offer now, nothing. Nothing to offer a man. It's too late now, at 68. He's going to have to cook for himself. I'm not cookin for him, washing. I'm not doing nothing. Now if he want to have me for himself some-time, O.K. But you see, I know wives are supposed to do more than that. You got duties at home for your husband. Keep his clothes clean. All that stuff. I can't do that no more. I been loose so long till I been set to my ways that I couldn't do it no more. I just likes to be out. I want to go and come when I get ready. I don't want no man to tell me nothin. I don't want no man no more.

They gave me a surprise party on my 72nd birthday which was August 29, 1981. Look at me. I sure was surprised.

139

Annie Mae Hunt and her family in Houston for a book signing.

My main subject is to treat people like I want to be treated.

ACKNOWLEDGEMENTS

I appreciate the advice and assistance by friends and colleagues who helped make this book possible: Frieda Werden, Eje Wray, Dr. Harvey G. Graff, Dr. Elneita Dever, Dr. Rose Brewer, Kirsten Grimstad, Peggy Kimball, Annie Chamberlain, Karyn London, Phyllis Harris, Janelle Scott, Mary Beth Rogers, Sherry Smith, and Ginger Jacobs.

The work of Willie Lee Gay, Ada Simond, Algerene Craig, Fannie Mae Lawless, and Dorothea Brown to illuminate the history of black women in Texas has been invaluable.

My children, Martha, Marc, and Debbie, have constantly encouraged and supported my efforts.

—Ruthe Winegarten

NOTES   by Ruthe Winegarten

Chapter 1

1 When was Mrs. Hunt's grandmother Tildy born? My guess is 1846–1849. If Tildy was 62 or 63 when Mrs. Hunt was born, then Tildy's year of birth was 1846 or 1847. If Tildy was 101 in 1947 when she died, then her birth year was 1846. Also see Note 14.

2 It is difficult to determine how Tildy got to Washington County. I was unable to reconstruct the time period or the route traveled. Some South Carolina "Boozies" could have brought Tildy to Mt. Pleasant, and then on to Washington County, where they kept her until Emancipation. Or she may have been sold by the "Boozies" to another family after they all arrived in Texas. Or Tildy could have been sold by some South Carolina "Boozies" to a family who took her to Texas.

3 There are three Southeast Texas counties important to Mrs. Hunt's story: historic Washington County (location of Brenham); Austin County (with the towns of Welcome and Industry); and Grimes County, location of Navasota. (The town of Wesley straddles the counties of Washington and Austin.) These counties were part of the Southern "Black Belt" where the plantation system was entrenched, and slavery was extremely profitable. At the beginning of the Civil War, one out of every four Texans was a slave, and most slaves lived in this plantation area which included the above three counties.

Stephen F. Austin led the first white settlers to Southeast Texas in 1821–22 when it was still part of Mexico. The Republic of Mexico had abolished slavery, but Austin was adept at getting interpretations of the Mexican law which allowed him and many of the other whites to bring along their own slaves, and to continue to buy and sell slaves. The Texas Declaration of Independence was proclaimed in Washington County in 1836 by a convention of white males, surrounded by their slaves and various Indian tribes. The "freedom-minded" delegates awarded about 4500 acres of land to "all persons, except Africans and their descendants, and Indians."

Before the Civil War, in 1850, Washington County had a large black population—47% of a total 6000. By 1870 the population had tripled, and blacks had increased to 55%. When Mrs. Hunt was born in 1909, blacks were again 47% of the total. From 1910 to 1980, the black population continued to decline, while the white population remained relatively stable. By 1980 only 22% of the total 21,651 population were black.

4 "Boozie" is the way Mrs. Hunt pronounced the name of Matilda's owners. Investigation has uncovered a number of similar-sounding names, but none connected with a Matilda. A James Bose was one of five commissioners named in 1846 to find the center of Titus County, location of Mt. Pleasant, where Tildy is supposed to have first landed from South Carolina with her owners. In Southeast Texas I found these family names: Boese, Bosse, Boozikee, Buscher, Buescher, Bossy, Bueseke, Bueske, Boelsche, Busse, and Boozer.

5 Mrs. Hunt explained that Matilda was a "Boozie," "cause when you were sold, you took whoever bought you, their name." However, slaves did not have last names. They were described in sales contracts and deeds by their first names, ages, and sometimes physical appearances. After Emancipation, some ex-slaves did take the last names of their first owners, and some took other names.

Also see Eugene D. Genovese, *Roll, Jordan, Roll*, New York: Vintage Books, 1976, pp. 443–450.

6 Mrs. Hunt said in a 1982 interview that her Grandmother Tildy's brothers and sisters were sold off first, and then her mother. Old Mistress seemed to have loved Tildy, but nevertheless she (or perhaps her husband) sold off Tildy's mother's children. This was a common practice. Lulu Wilson, an ex-slave, remembered: "I gets to thinkin' how Wash Hodges sold off Maw's chillen. He'd . . . have the folks come for 'em when my maw was in the fields. When she'd come back, she'd raise a ruckus. Then many the time I seed her plop right down to a settin' and cry about it. But she allowed there weren't nothing could be done, 'cause it's the slavery law. She said, 'Oh Lord, let me see the end of it before I die.'" (George P. Rawick, ed., *The American Slave: A Composite Autobiography*, 19 volumes. "Texas Narratives," vol. 10, part 9. Westport: Greenwood Pub. Co., 1979, p. 4191)

7 After Tildy was older, Sylvia, the daughter of one of her sisters, turned up. Tildy knew the name of the whites who had bought her sister, and was thus able to identify Sylvia as her niece. Said Mrs. Hunt, "Grandma's [Tildy's] niece [Sylvia] was her age, but she had children, and raised those children out there."

Chapter 2

8 This order, passed in the local court of Fayette County, which borders Washington County, was reprinted in F. Lotta, *Fayette County: Her History and Her People*, Schulenburg, Texas: by the author, Sticker Steam Press, 1902, pp. 136–137.

Lotta goes on to say, "The negro population did not cause any troubles in those times." Despite his statement and the passage of laws like the above, designed to terrorize the slave population, there were numerous instances of both individual and group resistance by Texas slaves from the 1820s to the end of the Civil War. Some slaves ran away to the Indians and to Mexico; some murdered their masters; and a few planned uprisings.

Chapter 3

9 Mrs. Hunt's uncle was part black, part white, and part Indian, but she calls him a "white man. That's all he was." Contrast this attitude with that of some whites who consider anyone with even the most distant black ancestor as black.

10 This type of gift was extremely rare. "Only a handful of ex-slaves were given farms in the early years of Reconstruction." (Roger L. Ransom and Richard Sutch, *One Kind of Freedom, the Economic Consequences of Emancipation*, Cambridge: Cambridge Univ. Press, 1977, p. 8) I have been unable to locate a deed for the period, 1860–1890, reflecting a transfer of land in Washington or Austin Counties from anyone whose name resembles Boozie to a Matilda Boozie or a Matilda Boozie Randon or an Eli Randon (her husband). However, Matilda and Eli had somehow acquired land by 1877. I did locate deeds reflecting purchases and sales of land by them in those counties by 1877 and later. See Note 17.

Chapter 4

11 Mrs. Hunt probably meant that her Grandfather Eli was part Seminole. We don't know how Eli got to Texas.

There was intermarriage or mixing between fugitive slaves and Indians, particularly among the Florida Seminoles, a peaceful tribe. The Seminoles committed only one offense in the eyes of the U.S. government—they welcomed runaway slaves. These Negroes were either taken as slaves by Seminole chiefs, or admitted into the tribe as free men and women.

Because of this policy, the U.S. government conducted its most costly and unnecessary Indian war against the Seminoles, resulting in their near extermination. The Seminoles signed a treaty, promising to vacate central Florida to the whites and receiving guarantees that those tribesmen who emigrated West could take their Negroes along. In the 1850s some Seminoles (including some blacks), who were exiled to the Western Country Territories (Arkansas), were led through Texas to freedom in Mexico. Others were captured by the Creeks and sold to whites. Eli may have been in one of these groups. (David G. Cooke, *Indians on the Warpath*, New York: Dodd Mead, 1957; Joshua Giddings, *The Exiles of Florida*, Columbus: Follett, Foster, 1858)

144

Mrs. Hunt said that her Grandmother Tildy was part Cherokee. The Cherokee Nation, numerous in South Carolina, also had runaway slaves among them, whom they enslaved. (*Reply of Colored Citizens of the Cherokee Nation to a Memorial of the Principal Chief and Cherokee Delegation, to the Commissioner of Indian Affairs, Praying for the Removal of Intruders from the Cherokee Nation*, Washington, D.C.: Downs & Brown, 1879) One of Tildy's ancestors could have been a slave of the Cherokees, and later resold to a white family.

handwritten note in margin: no mention of removal to Okla?

12 In 1977 Mrs. Hunt said that Matilda Boozie and Eli Randon were married in Navasota (on the Brazos River in Grimes County), but not by a court. In 1982 she said they were married in Washington County.

13 Eli Randon died in 1941. If he and Matilda married either at the end of the Civil War or shortly thereafter (1865–1870), they were married 75–80 years.

Chapter 5

14 Mrs. Hunt in a 1982 interview: "My grandmother said that Theodore [her first born] was 31 years old when he was killed in Brenham. He was strictly a lady's man—he cared about a man's wife. The man shot Theodore off his horse and his horse came home and he wasn't on it so Grandma knew then that something was the matter. She went looking for him. At that time, my mama Callie was about three or four years old." (Callie, Theodore's baby sister, was born in 1889, and thus Theodore died in 1892 or 1893. His year of birth was probably 1861 or 1862. If his mother, Tildy, was "near 13" when she got pregnant [see Chapter 3] and 13 or 14 when she gave birth to Theodore, then her year of birth could have been 1847, 1848, or 1849.)

15 After the Civil War, the agricultural land of the South was owned by the same whites who had owned both the land and the slaves before the war. Only a handful of ex-slaves like Matilda Boozie Randon were given farms in the early years of Reconstruction.

Large landowners divided their acreage into family-sized farms of 30 to 50 acres each and rented them to freedmen, either for a fixed rent (share tenants) or much more typically, for a share of the proceeds from the sale of the crop, usually one-half (sharecroppers).

In the case of the share tenants, like Pinky and her husband, the landlord provided only the land, housing, and fuel, and the tenants furnished animals, tools, and seed, and owned the crops which they produced. For the sharecroppers, the landlord furnished the land, housing, fuel, animals, wagons, tools, and seed, but not food, clothing or other necessities.

Both share tenants and sharecroppers usually ended up owing their souls to the country store. Neither group typically had enough start-up cash at the beginning of the growing season to buy food, clothing, etc., and therefore had to give the merchant a lien on their next year's crop to get credit, usually at a high interest rate. At the end of the season, when the merchant's books were settled against the return from the cash crop, the freedmen often ended up with no cash left to start the new year, and sometimes with a carry-over debt. (Ransom and Sutch, *One Kind of Freedom*, ibid., passim)

16 Texas common law has provided for untold years that in the sale of land, the owner may retain the mineral rights. Eli Randon was, perhaps, unaware of this right, or he may have sold most of his land before oil was discovered in Texas in 1901 (Spindletop), or before it was discovered in Washington County in 1912.

17 Eli Randon seems to have been a land trader. I found six deeds in the records of Washington and Austin counties, reflecting two land transactions in 1877, and one each in 1878, 1883, 1907, and 1916. For example, on February 23, 1877, Eli bought 110 acres of land in the forks of Mill Creek (Washington County) for $2090 in gold, giving the sellers five promissory notes at 10% interest, the first one of $418 being due the day after the sale. A year later he sold the same land for $1850, with $250 down, at 12% interest. He must have had sufficient capital to pay off the first note, and planned to make about $500 profit from the higher rate of interest. His wife Matilda's name shows up on several of the other deeds.

Chapter 6

18 During the 19th century and a good part of the 20th, most Texas women—native American, Hispanic, black, and Anglo—delivered their babies with the help of midwives. Midwifery has always been, and still is, legal in Texas.

19 Mrs. Hunt: "Those people down there cooked bread, cooked that bread, and Grandma'd bring bread home and we was there to gobble it up. We loved it. We called it light bread. Now what the 'light' means, I don't know. They'd make [mash] this stuff up and set it, it would rise up easy and rise up and you make it down again and after awhile you put it in your pan and put it in the stove. That loaf bread was called light bread."

Chapter 7

20 Mrs. Hunt's baby uncle Eli was not actually the baby of the family. He was the *neebaby* (next youngest to the baby). Mrs. Hunt's mother Callie was the baby.

Chapter 9

21 Delco lights were produced by a small home electric power plant used in rural areas in the 1918–1924 period. A power generator produced electricity for lights, water pumps, and home appliances. (Rachel Haggard, Delco-Remy Division, General Motors, Anderson, Indiana, telephone interview, October 4, 1982)

There probably exists a history of rural electrification

146

Chapter 13

22 "No county in Texas had a finer or more loyal colored population than that of Washington County. . . . They bought willingly of Liberty Bonds, sent their sons to the defense of our country during the last war. . ." (*Brenham Banner*, Historical Edition, 1934, v. 69, pp. 36–37)

Chapter 15

23 In the early 1920s American agriculture entered into a sharp and damaging depression. Prices of farm land and food fell, while almost all the costs of farming stayed the same or rose. At the same time, banks in the South and West cut back on credit issued to farmers. Thousands of tenant farmers, black and white, were either out of work or not earning enough to buy the basic necessities. (Russell Lord, *The Wallaces of Iowa*, Boston: Houghton Mifflin, 1947, p. 169, pp. 218–219)

24 Bud Jones was a black man who was apparently forced to do the bidding of Old Man Morrett, a white man. Said Mrs. Hunt: "Whatever Morrett say, Bud done. Old Man Morrett had Bud under some kind of spell or had something held over him. Now Bud Jones was his slave, some kind of slave."

25 Although there is no evidence that the attack on Annie Mae and her family was that of the Ku Klux Klan, the 1920s saw the KKK making a strong comeback in Texas. Their crimes of murder, rape, and arson were particularly numerous in Southeast Texas. In 1924 Ma Ferguson, the first woman ever elected governor, won office on an anti-Klan platform. Under her leadership the Legislature passed an anti-mask bill which finally crippled the Klan.

Chapter 17

26 See Alice Walker's characterization of Sophie in *The Color Purple*, New York and London: Harcourt, 1982.

Chapter 20

27 Mrs. George (Kate) Ripley started the first Texas birth control clinic in 1935—the Dallas Planned Parenthood Center, still in existence—although to do so was illegal. The federal Comstock Law prohibiting the dissemination of birth control information and devices was struck down in 1936.

28 This could be a holdover of propaganda originally aimed at female slaves by their owners and agents to encourage unlimited child bearing for profit. Lulu Wilson, an ex-slave, recalled; "Missus told me . . . if I'd marry she'd togger me up in a white dress and give me a weddin' supper. . . . I was 'bout thirteen or fourteen. . . . it weren't long after that when Missus Hodges got a doctor for me. The doctor told me lessen I had a baby, old as I was and married, I'd start in on spasms. So it weren't long till I had a baby." (George Rawick, ed., *The American Slave*,

"Texas Narratives," ibid., vol. 10, part 9, p. 4191) Another Texas slave, Mary Gaffney, defeated the ambition of her master to "raise him a lot more slaves . . . I cheated Maser. I never did have any slaves. . . I kept cotton roots and chewed them all the time but I was careful not to let Maser know or catch me. So I never did have any children while I was a slave. . . . Yes, after freedom, we had five children." (Rawick, ibid., vol. 5, part 4, p. 1453)

Chapter 21
29 Pickaninny usually refers to a small black child. It is probably a modification of the Portuguese word *pequinino,* meaning *very little,* or the Spanish word, *pequeño,* small.

Chapter 32
30 Originally payment of a state poll tax in Texas was a way of raising revenues, and was not required to vote. During the 1890s the Texas Populist Party threatened the control of the Democratic Party by electing a bloc of legislators and garnering a large vote in the governor's race. The Populists had reached their peak strength partly because they sought out and won the support of many black voters, formerly Republicans. In 1902 the Texas Legislature joined with those of nine other Southern states in making the payment of a poll tax a prerequisite for voting. In Texas, reasons given were to purify the ballot and prevent vote buying; to disfranchise the Negro; and to disfranchise Populist Party members, struggling farmers and laborers whose views were considered radical by some. As long as the poll tax, usually $1.50–$1.75, was required to vote, citizens' organizations like the NAACP and the League of Women Voters, particularly in the 1940s, 1950s, and early '60s, mounted "Pay your poll tax" campaigns to register as many persons as possible. In 1964 the 24th amendment to the U.S. Constitution abolished the poll tax as a prerequisite for federal elections, and in 1966, the poll tax was declared invalid as a voting requirement in state elections by a state constitutional amendment.

31 Funeral home owners in the black community have often been community leaders.

32 Mrs. Hunt explained that "some of the women in the projects had friends and those friends had good-lookin cars—not necessarily the women's."

33 In 1923 the Texas Legislature passed the "White Primary" law, excluding blacks from voting in the Democratic Party primary. (Women had gotten the right to vote in primaries only in 1918, and black women were still excluded in some counties.) Since Texas at that time was a one-party state, nomination in the primary was tantamount to election. Having been excluded from the white primary, blacks were shut out of the electoral process for all practical purposes until 1944 when the U.S. Supreme Court declared this law unconstitutional.

Chapter 33

34 Jim Mattox served as Congressman from Dallas County from 1976 to 1982 when he was elected Texas Attorney-General. Bill Bracklein was a state legislator; Larry Murdoch and Tom Ellis were Dallas County district clerks. Sheriff Clarence Jones served in the 1970s; Earle Cabell was a Congressman from 1964 to 1972.

35 Eddie Bernice Johnson was the first black woman to serve in the Texas Legislature from Dallas County—1973–1977. She played a key role in Jimmy Carter's 1976 Texas presidential campaign. In 1977, President Carter appointed her as director of the Dallas regional office, Department of Health, Education, and Welfare (HEW); later she was promoted to be Special Assistant in the national HEW office. She later served as a Texas State Senator until her election to the U.S. Congress from Dallas County in 1993.

36 Sarah T. Hughes served in the Texas Legislature from 1931 to 1935, when she was appointed as Texas' first female district judge. In 1961 Judge Hughes was named U.S. judge for Texas' Northern District by President John F. Kennedy, an office she still holds.

37 Eddie Bernice Johnson used her last opportunity as an outgoing Democratic member of the state House of Representatives to make a political endorsement.

Chapter 34

38 The Democratic Women of Dallas County was organized in 1920.

39 The Texas Black Caucus, meeting annually, brings together the top black political leaders. Founded in 1978, its major goals are to enhance the political consciousness of the black community through education and candidate endorsements.

40 Mrs. Hunt explained that criticisms from the churchgoers intimidated some people from voting.

PHOTOGRAPH CREDITS

All of the photographs are from the scrapbooks of Annie Mae Hunt and her children, except for those on the following pages:

iii (title page): By Diana Dring
vii: By Eje W. Wray
viii: Top left, by Ruthe Winegarten; top right, photographer unknown; bottom right, by Ruthe Winegarten; bottom left, Winegarten scrapbook
x: Top, by Ruthe Winegarten; others, Winegarten scrapbook
xiii: Photos by Walter Griffin; article, Winegarten scrapbook
xiv: Articles, Winegarten scrapbook; photos by Winegarten
xvi: By Steve Jones/Light and Lead Images
1: Top two, by Danna Byrom; bottom, by Tomás Pantin
2: By Diana Dring
4: Top, by Eje W. Wray; bottom, courtesy Sam W. Russell; copied from Traylor Russell, *Pioneers and Heroes of Titus County* (Waco: Rotary Club of Mt. Pleasant, 1974)
6: Art work by Eje W. Wray
8: By Walter Griffin
14: By Earl Dotter
15, 17: By Eje W. Wray
20: The Woman's Collection, Texas Woman's University, Denton
24: University of Texas Institute of Texan Cultures, Z-1569
28: By Eje W. Wray
30: George Washington Carver Museum, Austin
31: Collection of Eje W. Wray
36: By Russell Lee; courtesy Photographs and Prints Division, Schomburg Center for Research in Black Culture, The New York Public Library, Astor, Lenox, and Tilden Foundations
38: By Dorothea Lange; courtesy Photographs and Prints Division, Schomburg Center for Research in Black Culture, The New York Public Library, Astor, Lenox, and Tilden Foundations
40: Top, Hunt scrapbook; bottom, by Eje W. Wray
44: Top, by Eje W. Wray; bottom, Hunt scrapbook
48: By Jack Lewis, Texas Department of Transportation
52, 54, 66: By Diana Dring
82: By Eje W. Wray
86: Top, by Eje W. Wray; bottom, by Diana Dring
88, 90–91: By Eje W. Wray
92: Top, courtesy of Willie Lee Gay; bottom, Hunt scrapbook
94: By Dewitt Humphrey, courtesy of Bernice Humphrey
96: By Ruthe Winegarten

98: By Mike Boroff ©*Austin American-Statesman*
112: By Diana Dring
119: By Ruthe Winegarten
120: Top, by Ruthe Winegarten; bottom, Hunt scrapbook
125, 130: By Eje W. Wray
132: Top, by Eje W. Wray; bottom, Hunt scrapbook
134: By Eje W. Wray
140: By James Kibble
152: By Danna Byrom

I am Annie Mae

A One-Woman Musical Play by Naomi Carrier and Ruthe Winegarten.

I Am Annie Mae, an exhilarating one-woman musical based on this book, unfolds through gospel, jazz, blues, rock & roll and field chants. In two acts, the legacy of Annie Mae Hunt and her family has been transformed into an entertaining and inspirational production that has delighted audiences of all ages. It makes you laugh, it makes you cry, it leaves you humming the tune of its energy and spirit.

Twenty songs from powerful lament to sassy slapstick form the heart of the musical. Threaded together by narration, they tell the story of Annie Mae in a stirring song and dance celebration.

Singer/actress Belinda Simmons stars as Annie Mae, accompanied by composer/lyricist Naomi Carrier on the piano. The show is suitable for staging in theaters, auditoriums, museum galleries, lobbies and a range of non-traditional dramatic venues. It is designed to be infinitely adaptable, with little need for technical support.